EDGAR LEE
MASTERS
AMERICAN POET

UNITED STATES 6¢

THE GREAT VALLEY

THE MACMILLAN COMPANY
NEW YORK · BOSTON · CHICAGO · DALLAS
ATLANTA · SAN FRANCISCO

MACMILLAN & CO., Limited
LONDON · BOMBAY · CALCUTTA
MELBOURNE

THE MACMILLAN CO. OF CANADA, Ltd.
TORONTO

THE GREAT VALLEY

By

EDGAR LEE MASTERS

AUTHOR OF "SPOON RIVER ANTHOLOGY"
"SONGS AND SATIRES," ETC.

New York
THE MACMILLAN COMPANY
1916

Norwood Press
J. S. Cushing Co. — Berwick & Smith Co.
Norwood, Mass., U.S.A.

TO THE MEMORY

OF

SQUIRE DAVIS AND LUCINDA MASTERS

WHO, CLOSE TO NATURE, ONE IN DEEP RELIGIOUS FAITH, THE OTHER
IN PANTHEISTIC RAPTURE AND HEROISM, LIVED NEARLY A
HUNDRED YEARS IN THIS LAND OF ILLINOIS

I INSCRIBE

THE GREAT VALLEY

IN ADMIRATION OF THEIR GREAT STRENGTH, MASTERY
OF LIFE, HOPEFULNESS, CLEAR AND
BEAUTIFUL DEMOCRACY

EDGAR LEE MASTERS

CONTENTS

	PAGE
FORT DEARBORN	1
CAPT. JOHN WHISTLER	5
EMILY BROSSEAU: IN CHURCH	12
THE OUIJA BOARD	19
HANGING THE PICTURE	21
LINCOLN AND DOUGLAS DEBATES	26
AUTOCHTHON	33
GRANT AND LOGAN AND OUR TEARS	43
THE MUNICIPAL PIER	49
GOBINEAU TO TREE	53
OLD PIERY	60
THE TYPICAL AMERICAN?	68
COME, REPUBLIC	72
PAST AND PRESENT	76
ROBERT G. INGERSOLL	77
AT HAVANA	78
THE MOURNER'S BENCH	80
THE BAY WINDOW	83
MAN OF OUR STREET	90
ACHILLES DEATHERIDGE	93
SLIP SHOE LOVEY	95

CONTENTS

	PAGE
THE ARCHANGELS	98
SONG OF CHANGE	101
MEMORABILIA	102
TO A SPIROCHÆTA	104
CATO BRADEN	106
WINSTON PRAIRIE	120
WILL BOYDEN LECTURES	125
THE DESPLAINES FOREST	129
THE GARDEN	131
THE TAVERN	134
O SAEPE MECUM	138
MALACHY DEGAN	141
MY DOG PONTO	144
THE GOSPEL OF MARK	147
MARSYAS	154
WORLDS BACK OF WORLDS	160
THE PRINCESS' SONG	164
THE FURIES	166
APOLLO AT PHERÆ	168
STEAM SHOVEL CUT	173
THE HOUSES	178
THE CHURCH AND THE HOTEL	185
SUSIE	188
HAVING HIS WAY	190
THE ASP	198
THE FAMILY	206
THE SUBWAY	207
THE RADICAL'S MESSAGE	211
BOMBYX	216
THE APOLOGY OF DEMETRIUS	218

CONTENTS

		PAGE
A Play in Four Acts	.	224
Theodore Dreiser	.	228
John Cowper Powys	.	231
New Year's Day	.	234
Playing Blind	.	240
I Shall Never See You Again	.	241
Elizabeth to Monsieur D——	.	244
Monsieur D—— to the Psychoanalyst . . .	.	249
The Last Confession	.	261
In the Loggia	.	268
Be With Me Through the Spring	.	272
Desolate Scythia	.	273
The Search	.	274

THE GREAT VALLEY

I

FORT DEARBORN

Here the old Fort stood
When the river bent southward.
Now because the world pours itself into Chicago
The Lake runs into the river
Past docks and switch-yards,
And under bridges of iron.

Sand dunes stretched along the lake for miles.
There was a great forest in the Loop.
Now Michigan Avenue lies
Between miles of lights,
And the Rialto blazes
Where the wolf howled.

In the loneliness of the log-cabin,
Across the river,
The fur-trader played his fiddle
When the snow lay
About the camp of the Pottawatomies
In the great forest.
Now to the music of the Kangaroo Hop,
And Ragging the Scale,

And La Seduccion,
The boys and girls are dancing
In a cafe near Lake Street.

The world is theirs now.
There is neither a past nor a to-morrow,
Save of dancing.
Nor do they know that behind them
In the seed not yet sown
There are eyes which will open upon Chicago,
And feet which will blossom for the dance,
And hands which will reach up
And push them into the silence
Of the old fiddler.

They threw a flag
Over the coffin of Lieutenant Farnum
And buried him back of the Fort
In ground where now
The spice mills stand.
And his little squaw with a baby
Sat on the porch grieving
While the band played.
Then hands pushing the world
Buried a million soldiers and afterward
Pale multitudes swept through the Court-house
To gaze for the last time
Upon the shrunken face of Lincoln.

FORT DEARBORN

And the fort at thirty-fifth street vanished.
And where the Little Giant lived
They made a park
And put his statue
Upon a column of marble.
Now the glare of the steel mills at South Chicago
Lights the bronze brow of Douglas.
It is his great sorrow
Haunting the Lake at mid-night.

When the South was beaten
They were playing
John Brown's body lies mouldering in the Grave,
And Babylon is Fallen and Wake Nicodemus.
Now the boys and girls are dancing
To the Merry Whirl and Hello Frisco
Where they waltzed in crinoline
When the Union was saved.

There was the Marble Terrace
Glory of the seventies!
They wrecked it,
And brought colors and figures
From later Athens and Pompeii
And put them on walls.
And beneath panels of red and gold,
And shimmering tesseræ,
And tragic masks and comic masks,

And wreaths and bucrania,
Upon mosaic floors
Red lipped women are dancing
With dark men.
Some sit at tables drinking and watching,
Amorous in an air of French perfumes.

Like ships at mid-night
The kingdoms of the world
Know not whither they go nor to what port.
Nor do you, embryo hands,
In the seed not yet sown
Know of the wars to come.

They may fill the sky with armored dragons
And the waters with iron monsters;
They may build arsenals
Where now upon marble floors
The boys and girls
Are dancing the Alabama Jubilee,
The processional of time is a falling stream
Through which you thrust your hand.
And between the dancers and the silence forever
There shall be the livers
Gazing upon the torches they have lighted,
And watching their own which are failing,
And crying for oil,
And finding it not!

II

CAPTAIN JOHN WHISTLER

*(Captain John Whistler built Fort Dearborn in 1803.
His son, George Washington, who was an engineer
and built a railroad in Russia for the Czar in 1842,
was the father of the artist, James Abbott McNeill
Whistler.)*

Throw logs upon the fire! Relieve the guard
At the main gate and wicket gate! Lieutenant
Send two men 'round the palisades, perhaps
They'll find some thirsty Indians loitering
Who may think there is whiskey to be had
After the wedding. Get my sealing wax!
Now let me see "November, eighteen four:
Dear Jacob: On this afternoon my daughter
Was married to James Abbott, it's the first
Wedding of white people in Chicago —
That's what we call Fort Dearborn now and then.
They left at once on horseback for Detroit."
The "Tracy" will sail in to-morrow likely.
"To Jacob Kingsbury"— that's well addressed.
Don't fail to give this letter to the captain,
That it may reach Detroit ere they do.
I wonder how James Abbott and my Sarah
Will fare three hundred miles of sand and marsh,

[5]

And tangled forest in this hard November?
More logs upon the fire! The mist comes down!
The lake roars like a wind, and not a star
Lights up the blackness. They have almost reached
The Calumet by now. Good luck James Abbott!
I'm glad my Sarah wed so brave a man,
And one so strong of arm.

                    It's eighteen four,
It's almost eighteen five. It's twenty years
Since I was captured when Burgoyne was whipped
At Saratoga. Why, it's almost twenty
Since I became an American soldier. Now
Here am I builder of this frontier fort,
And its commander! Aged now forty-nine.
But in my time a British soldier first,
Now an American; first resident
Of Ireland, then England, Maryland,
Now living here. I see the wild geese fly
To distant shores from distant shores and wonder
How they endure such strangeness. But what's that
To man's adventures, change of home, what's that
To my unsettled life? Why there's La Salle:
They say La Salle in sixteen seventy-one
Was here, and now it's almost eighteen five.
And what's your wild geese to La Salle! He's born
At Rouen, sails the seas, and travels over
Some several thousand miles through Canada.

CAPTAIN JOHN WHISTLER

Is here exploring portages and rivers.
Ends up at last down by the Rio Grande,
And dies almost alone half way around
The world from where he started.   There's a man!
May some one say of me: There was a man! . . .

I'm lonely without Sarah, without James.
Tom bring my pipe and that tobacco bag.
Here place my note to Jacob Kingsbury
There on the shelf — remember, to the captain
When the "Tracy" comes.   Draw, boys, up to the fire
I'll tell you what a wondrous dream I had,
And woke with on my Sarah's wedding day. . . .

I had an uncle back in Ireland
Who failed at everything except his Latin.
He could spout Virgil till your head would ache.
And when I was a boy he used to roll
The Latin out, translating as he went:
The ghost of Hector comes before Æneas,
And warns him to leave Troy.   His mother Venus
Tells him to settle in another land!
The Delphic oracle misunderstood,
Æneas goes to Crete.   He finds at last
His ships are fired by the Trojan women,
Great conflagration!   Down he goes to hell,
And then the Sibyl shows him what's to be:
What race of heroes shall descend from him,

[7]

And how a city's walls he shall up-build
In founding Rome. . . .

                So last night in my dream
This uncle came to me and said to me:
"'Aeneas' Whistler you shall found a city.
You've built Fort Dearborn, that is the beginning.
Imperial Rome could be put in a corner
Of this, the city which you'll found.   Fear not
The wooden horse, but have a care for cows:
I see ships burning on your muddy Tiber,
And toppling walls."   I dreamed I felt the heat.
But then a voice said "Where's your little boy
George Washington?" — come sit on father's knee,
And hear about my dream — there little boy!
Well, as I said, I felt the heat and then
I felt the cruelest cold and then the voice:
"You cannot come to Russia with your boy,
He'll make his way."   I woke up with these words,
And found the covers off and I was cold.
And then no sooner did I fall asleep
Than this old uncle re-appeared and said:
"A race of heroes shall descend from you,
Here shall a city stand greater than Rome."
With that he seemed to alter to a witch,
A woman's form, the voice of him changed too,
And said: "I'm Mother Shipton, Captain Whistler.
"Men through the mountains then shall ride,

[8]

CAPTAIN JOHN WHISTLER

"Nor horse nor ass be by their side" —
Think, gentlemen, what it would be to ride
In carriages propelled by steam! And then
This dream became a wonder in a wonder
Of populous streets, of flying things, of spires
Of driven mist that looked like fiddle strings
From tree to tree. Of smoke-stacks over-topping
The tallest pine; of bridges built of levers,
And such a haze of smoke, and cloud like shapes
Passing along like etchings one by one:
Cathedrals, masts as thick as hazel thickets,
And buildings great as hills, and miles of lights.
Till by some miracle the sun had moved,
And rose not in the east but in the south.
And shone along the shore line of the Lake,
As he shines o'er the Lake when he arises,
And makes an avenue of gold, no less
This yellow sand took glory of his light.
And where he shone it seemed an avenue,
And over it, where now the dunes stretch south,
Along the level shore of sand, there stood
These giant masses, etchings as it were!
And Mother Shipton said: "This is your city.
"A race of heroes shall descend from you;
"Your son George Washington shall do great deeds.
"And if he had a son what would you name him?"
Well, as I went to sleep with thoughts of Sarah
And praises for James Abbott, it was natural

That I should say "I'd name him after James."
"Well done" said Mother Shipton and then van-
    ished. . . .
I woke to find the sun-light in my room,
And from my barracks window saw the Lake
Stirred up to waves slate-colored by the wind;
Some Indians loitering about the fort.
They knew this was James Abbott's wedding day,
And Sarah's day of leaving.

                            Soldiers! Comrades!
What is most real, our waking hours, our dreams?
Where was I in this sleep? What are our dreams
But lands which lie below our hour's horizon,
Yet still are seen in a reflecting sky,
And which through earth and heaven draw us on?
Look at me now! Consider of yourselves:
Housed, fed, yet lonely, in this futile task
By this great water, in this waste of grass,
Close to this patch of forest, on this river
Where wolves howl, and the Indian waits his chance —
Consider of your misery, your sense
Of worthless living, living to no end:
I tell you no man lives but to some end.
He may live only to increase the mass
Wherewith Fate is borne-down, or just to swell
The needed multitude when the hero passes,
To give the hero heart! But every man

CAPTAIN JOHN WHISTLER

Walks, though in blindness, to some destiny
Of human growth, who only helps to fill,
And helps that way alone, the empty Fate
That waits for lives to give it Life.

                                    And look
Here are we housed and fed, here is a fire
And here a bed. A hundred years ago
Marquette, La Salle, scarce housed and poorly fed
Gave health and life itself to find the way
Through icy marshes, treacherous swamps and forests
For this Fort Dearborn, where to-night we sit
Warming ourselves against a roaring hearth.
And what's our part? It is not less than theirs.
And what's the part of those to come? Not less
Than ours has been! And what's the life of man?
To live up to the God in him, to obey
The Voice which says: You shall not live and rest.
Nor sleep, nor mad delight nor senses fed,
Nor memory dulled, nor tortured hearing stopped
To drown my Voice shall leave you to forget
Life's impulse at the heart of Life, to strive
For men to be, for cities, nobler states
Moving foreshadowed in your dreams at night,
And realized some hundred years to come.
When this Fort Dearborn, you and all of you,
And I who sit with pipe and son on knee,
Regretting a dear daughter, who this hour

THE GREAT VALLEY

Is somewhere in the darkness (like our souls
Which move in darkness, listening to the beat
Of our mysterious hearts, or with closed eyes
Sensing a central Purpose) shall be dust —
Our triumphs, sorrows, even our names forgotten.
And all we knew lost in the wreck and waste
And change of things.   And even what we did
For cities, nobler states, and greater men
Forgotten too.   It matters not.   We work
For cities, nobler states and greater men,
Or else we die in Life which is the death
Which soldiers must not die!

III

EMILY BROSSEAU: IN CHURCH

*Domine, Jesu Christe, Rex gloriae, libera animas omnium
    fidelium defunctorum de poenis inferni, et de pro-
    fundo lacu.*

Leave me now and I will watch here through the night,
And I'll put in new candles, if these fail.
I'll sit here as I am, where I can see
His brow, his nose's tip and thin white hair,
And just beyond his brow, above the altar,
The red gash in the side of Jesus like
A candle's flame when burning to the socket.
Go all of you, and leave me.   I don't care

EMILY BROSSEAU: IN CHURCH

How cold the church grows.   Michael Angelo
Went to a garret, which was cold, and stripped
His feet, and painted till the chill of death
Took hold of him, a man just eighty-seven,
And I am ninety, what's the odds? — go now . . .

Now Jean we are alone!   Your very stillness
Is like intenser life, as in your brow
Your soul was crystallized and made more strong,
And nearer to me.   You are here, I feel you.
I close my eyes and feel you, you are here.
Therefore a little talk before the dawn,
Which will come soon.   Dawn always comes too soon
In times like this.   It waits too long in times
Of absence, and you will be absent soon. . . .

I want to talk about my happiness,
My happy life, the part you played in it.
There never was a day you did not kiss me
Through nearly seventy years of married life.
I had two hours of heaven in my life.
The first one was the dance where first we met.
The other when last fall they brought me roses,
Those ninety roses for my birth-day, when
They had me tell them of the first Chicago
I saw when just a child, about the Fort;
The cabins where the traders lived, who worked,
And made the fortune of John Jacob Astor.

Poor Jean! It's scarce a week since you were struck.
You sat down in your chair, 'twas after dinner,
Then suddenly I saw your head fall forward.
You could not speak when I went over to you.
But afterwards when you were on the bed
I leaned above you and you took the ribbon,
That hung down from my cap and pressed it trembling
Against your lips. What triumph in your death!
Your death was like a mass, mysterious, rich
Like Latin which the priests sing and the choir —
May angels take you and with Lazarus,
Once poor, receive you to eternal rest. . . .
Two hours of heaven in my life that's true!
And years between that made life more than good.
My first sight of Chicago stands for all
My life became for you and all I've lived.
The year is 1829, you know of course.
I've told you of the trip in Prairie schooners
From Ft. Detroit round the lake, we camped
Along the way, the last time near the place
Where Gary and the steel mills are to-day.
And the next morning what a sky! as blue
As a jay's wing, with little rifts of snow
Along the hollows of the yellow dunes,
And some ice in the lake, which lapped a little,
And purplish colors far off in the north.
So round these more than twenty miles we drove
That April day. And when we came as far

As thirty-ninth or thirty-first perhaps —
Just sand hills then — I never can forget it —
What should I see? Fort Dearborn dazzling bright,
All newly white-washed right against that sky,
And the log cabins round it, far away
The rims of forests, and between a prairie
With wild flowers in the grasses red and blue —
Such wild flowers and such grasses, such a sky,
Such oceans of sweet air, in which were rising
Straight up from Indian wigwams spires of smoke,
About where now the Public Library stands
On Randolph Street. And as we neared the place
There was the flag, a streaming red and white
Upon a pole within the Fort's inclosure.
I cried for happiness though just a child,
And cry now thinking. . . .

                     I must set this candle
To see your pale brow better! What's the hour?
The night is passing, and I have so much
To say to you before the dawn. . . .

                          Well, then
The first hour that I call an hour of heaven:
Who was that man that built the first hotel? —
It stood across the river from the Fort —
No matter. But before that I had heard
Nothing beside a fiddle, living here

[15]

Amid the traders eleven years or so.
And this man for his hotel's opening
Had brought an orchestra from somewhere.   Think
Bass viols, violins, and horns and flutes.
I'm dressed up like a princess for those days.
I'm sixteen years of age and pass the door,
Enter the ball-room where such candle-light
As I had never seen shone on me, they
Bored sockets in suspended wheels of wood
And hung them from the ceiling, chandeliers!
And at that moment all the orchestra
Broke into music, yes, it was a waltz!
And in that moment — what a moment-full!
This hotel man presented you and said
You were my partner for the evening.   Jean
I call this heaven, for its youth and love!
I'm sixteen and you're twenty and I love you.
I slip my arm through yours for you to lead me,
You are so strong, so ruddy, kind and brave.
I want you for a husband, for a friend,
A guide, a solace, father to the child
That I can bear.   Oh Jean how can I talk so
In this lone church at mid-night of such things,
With all these candles burning round your face.
I who have rounded ninety-years, and look
On what was sweet, long seventy years ago?
Feeling this city even at mid-night move
In restlessness, desire, around this church,

EMILY BROSSEAU: IN CHURCH

Where once I saw the prairie grass and flowers;
And saw the Indians in their colored trappings
Pour from a bottle of whisky on the fire
A tribute to the Spirit of the world,
And dance and sing for madness of that Spirit?

Well, Jean, my other hour.   I've spoken before
Of our long life together glad and sad,
But mostly good.   I'm happy for it all.
This other hour is marked, I call it heaven
Just as I told you, not because they stood
Around me as a mystery from the past,
And looked at me admiringly for my age,
My strength in age, my life that spanned the growth
Of my Chicago from a place of huts,
Just four or five, a fort, and all around it
A wilderness, to what it is this hour
Where most three million souls are living, nor
Because I saw this rude life, and beheld
The World's Fair where such richnesses of time
Were spread before me — not because of these,
Nor for the ninety roses, nor the tribute
They paid me in them, nor their gentle words —
These did not make that hour a heaven, no —
Jean, it was this:

          First I was just as happy
As I was on that night we danced together.

And that I could repeat that hour's great bliss
At ninety years, though in a different way,
And for a different cause, that was the thing
That made me happy.   For you see it proves,
Just give the soul a chance it's happiness
Is endless, let the body house it well,
Or house it ill, but give it but a chance
To speak itself, not stifle it, or hush it
With hands of flesh against the quivering strings,
Made sick or weak by time, the soul will find
Delights as good as youth has to the end.
And even if the flesh be sick there's Heine:
Few men had raptures keen as his, though lying
With death beside him through a stretch of years.
It must be something in the soul as well,
Which makes me think a third hour shall be mine
In spite of death, yes Jean it must be so!
I want that third hour, I shall pray for it
Unceasingly, I want it for my soul's sake:
Which will have happiness in its very power
And dignity that time nor change can hurt.
For if I have it you shall have it too.
And in that third hour we shall give each other
Something that's kindred to the souls we gave
That night we danced together — but much more! . .

It's dawn!   Good bye till then, my Jean, good bye!

IV

THE OUIJA BOARD

(David Kennison died in Chicago February 24th, 1852, aged 115 years, 3 months and 17 days. Veteran of the Revolution.)

David Kennison is here born at Kingston in the year
  Seventeen thirty-seven and it's nineteen sixteen now,
Dumped the tea into the harbor, saw Cornwallis'
  career
    End at Yorktown with the sullen thunder written
    on his brow.

Was at West Point when the traitor Arnold gave up
    the fort,
  Saw them hang Major Andre for a spy and his due.
Settled down in Sackett's Harbor for a rest of a sort,
    Till I crossed the western country in the year forty-
    two.

And I saw Chicago rising in the ten years to come,
  Ere I passed in the fifties to the peace of the dead.
Now where is there a city in the whole of Christendom
    Where such roar is and such walking is around a
    grave's head?

Oh, 'twas fighting as a soldier in the wars of the land;
  And 'twas giving and living to make the people free
That kept me past a century an oak to withstand
    The heat and snow and weevils that break down a
    tree.

There were other dead around me with a slab to mark
    When they heaped the final pillow for my honor's
    meed.
Now the lovers stopping curiously in Lincoln Park
    Look at the bronze tablet on my boulder and read:

How I fought at Long Island and fought at White
    Plains —
    What does it mean you lovers who scan what is
    scored
On the tablet on my boulder?—Why the task remains
    To make the torch brighter and to keep clean the
    sword.

Go labor for the future.   Go make the cities great:
    There are other realms to conquer for the men to
    be.
For it's toil and it's courage that solve a soul's fate,
    And it's giving and living that make a people free!

V

HANGING THE PICTURE

Before you pull that string,
And strip away that veil,
I rise to enter my objection
To the hanging of Archer Price's picture
Here in this hall. . . .
For I'll venture the artist has tried to soften
The vain and shifty look of the eyes;
And the face that looked like a harte-beest's,
And the rabbit mouth that looked like a horse's,
Lipping oats from a leather bag!

I knew this man in '28
When he drifted here from Maine, he said.
And now it's eighteen ninety two:
This year is sacred to conquerors,
Discoverers and soldiers.
And I object to the hanging of pictures
Of men who trade while others fight,
And follow the army to get the loot,
And rest till other men are tired,
Then grab the spoils while the workers sleep.
I would like to burn all masks,
And padded shoes,
And smash all dark lanterns.

THE GREAT VALLEY

And take all friends of the people
And brand them with the letter "B,"
Which means "Betrayer."
And I would like to enter the Kingdom of Heaven
Just to see the publicans who will be there,
And the Archer Prices who will not be there!

You call him a great man,
And a prophetic man,
And a leader, and a savior,
And a man who was wise in an evil world
Of tangled interests and selfish power,
And who knew the art of compromise,
And how to get half when you can't get all!
You haven't probed deep enough in this man.
For he was great as the condor is great.
And prophetic as the wolf is prophetic.
And a leader as the jackal is a leader.
And his wisdom was that of the python,
Which will swallow a hare when no pig is at hand!

He was rich,
He was well known,
His name was linked with lofty things,
And adorned all noble committees.
And he was a friend of art and music —
He gave them money!
He was on the Library Board,

HANGING THE PICTURE

And the Commerce Board, and every board
For building up the city —
I admit these things.   They were pawns on the board
    for him.
That's why I rise to enter my objection
To hanging his picture here!

We had no telephones in those days.
But there was a certain man of power,
A man who was feared, as one might fear
A lion that hides in the jungle.
And this man sat in a hidden room
As a banded-epira waits and watches.
And he went from this room to his house in a cab,
And back to this room in a cab.
But everyone knew that Archer Price
Was doing the will of the man in the room,
Though you never saw the two together,
As you never could see together the leaders
Of some of these late bi-partisan deals.
But Archer Price was so much alike
This secret man in the room;
And did so much what we knew
He wanted done, and built the city
So near to the heart's desire of this man
That all of us knew that the two conferred
In spite of the fact that telephones
Had never been heard of then. . . .

THE GREAT VALLEY

Well, because of this man in the room,
As well as because of Price himself,
Everyone feared him, no one knew
Exactly how to fight him.
Everyone hated him, although
Everyone helped him to wealth and power.
He was what you'd call a touch-me-not.
If you clodded him you ran the risk
Of hitting the teacher, or maybe a child.
He always walked with the wind to his back:
If you spit at him it would fly in your face.
And though we suspected more than we knew
Of his subtle machinations,
No.one could attack him for what was known.
Because the things he was known to be doing
Were service to those, who couldn't allow
The service to be imperiled.

There never was a time
This man was out of public office.
He clung to the people's treasury
As a magnet clings to a magnet.
Why didn't your orator tell this audience
He started in life as town assessor?
That would have left me with nothing to say
Except he traded the fixing of taxes
For business!
Oh, you people who unveil pictures!

[24]

HANGING THE PICTURE

In his day no one was permitted to say this.
And now everyone has forgotten it.
It is useless to say it.
And here in the year of Columbus
You are unveiling his picture!

And you say the Illinois and Michigan Canal
Had never been built or saved for the people
Except for Archer Price!
Why don't you tell that he fought the Canal in 1830,
Saying it would burden the people?
And why don't you say that even then
He was acting for his own interests and the man in the
    room?
Why don't you show that his art of compromise
Created the Public Canal Committee
When he failed to block the Canal,
And failed of appointment as Canal Commissioner?
Why don't you show that through that committee
The squatters stole the wharves on the river?
Why don't you show how his friends grew rich
Through buying the lands at public sales
Which were given to build the Canal,
And which the Committee was pretending to conserve?
Why don't you show that through that Committee,
Pretending to be a friend of the people,
He opened a fight at length on the squatters
And won the fight, and won the wharves

For himself and a clique of friends?
Why don't you tell —?

> Cry me down if you will —

I object — I object —

VI

THE LINCOLN AND DOUGLAS DEBATES

Have you ever seen the Douglas monument
There in Chicago?
They say it's by the Lake,
With a column of marble a hundred feet high,
And a statue of The Little Giant on top,
With knit brows and lion face,
Like he used to look when debatin' with Linkern.
I want to go up to Chicago sometime,
To see that monument.

And some one told me
They carved on his marble coffin the words:
"Tell my children to obey the laws,
And uphold the constitution."
Well, they couldn't have put sadder words
On his coffin than that.
For it was tryin' to obey the laws and support the
constitution
That killed him.
And why should his children do the same thing and die?

THE LINCOLN AND DOUGLAS DEBATES

You young men of this day don't care,
And you don't understand the old questions.
But a man's life is always worth understanding,
Especially a man's like The Little Giant.
Now this was the point:
There was that devilish thing slavery,
And The Little Giant, as senator,
Put through a bill for leaving it to the people
Whether they would have slavery in Kansas or Ne-
    braska,
Or any other territory, and that was popular sover-
    eignty —
And sounds democratic; but three years later
Along comes the Supreme Court and says:
The people of a territory must have slavery
Whether they want it or not, because
The constitution is for slavery, and it follows the flag!
Well, there was The Little Giant
Caught between the law and the constitution!
And tryin' to obey 'em both!
Or better still he was like Lem Reese's boy
Who was standin' one time one foot on shore,
And one in a skiff, baitin' a hook,
And all at once Col. Lankford's little steamer
Came along and bobbled the skiff;
And it started to glide out into the river, —
Why the boy walked like a spread compass
For a month.

For the skiff was movin', and that's the law.
And his other foot slipped on the slimy bank,
And that's the constitution!

But if you want to consider a minute
How Time plays tag with people,
And how no one can tell
When he'll be It, just think:
There was Bill McKinley
Who kept the old constitution's from goin' to the
        Philippines,
And they elected him.
And here was The Little Giant,
Who wanted to send it everywhere,
And they defeated him.
So you see it depends on what it means
Whether you want to keep it or send it.
And nobody knows what it means —
Not even judges.

But just the same them were great days.
One time The Little Giant came here with Linkern
And talked from the steps of the Court-house;
And you never saw such a crowd of people:
Democrats, Whigs, and Locofocos,
Know-nothings and Anti-masonics,
Blue lights, Spiritualists, Republicans
Free Soilers, Socialists, Americans — such a crowd.

THE LINCOLN AND DOUGLAS DEBATES

Linkern's voice squeaked up high,
And didn't carry.
But Douglas!
People out yonder in Proctor's Grove,
A mile from the Court House steps,
Could hear him roar and hear him say:
"I'm going to trot him down to Egypt
And see if he'll say the things he says
To the black republicans in northern Illinois."
It made you shiver all down your spine
To see that face and hear that voice —
And that was The Little Giant!

And then on the other hand there was
Abe Linkern standing six foot four,
As thin as a rail, with a high-keyed voice,
And sometimes solemn, and sometimes comic
As any clown you ever saw,
And runnin' Col. Lankford's little steamer,
As it were, you know, which would bobble the skiff,
Which was the law; and The Little Giant's other foot
Would slip on the bank, which was the constitution.
And you could almost hear him holler "ouch."
And Linkern would say: This argument
Of the Senator's is thin as soup
Made from the shadow of a starved pigeon!
And then the crowd would yell, and the cornet band
Would play, and men would walk away and say:

Linkern floored him. And others would say:
He aint no match for The Little Giant.
But I'll declare if I could decide
Which whipped the other.
For to let the people decide whether they wanted
    slavery
Sounded good.
And to have the constitution in force sounded good.
And not to have any slavery at all sounded good.
But so far as the law was concerned,
And where it was, and what you could do with it
It was like the shell game:
Now you see the little ball and now you don't!
Who's got a dollar to say where the little ball is?

But when you try to obey the laws and support the
    constitution,
It reminds me of a Campbellite preacher
We had here years ago.
And he debated with the Methodist preacher
As to whether immersion or sprinkling
Was the way to salvation.
And the Campbellite preacher said:
"The holy scripture says:
'And Jesus when he was baptised
Went up straightway out of the water.'
And how could he come up out of the water
If he wasn't in?" asked the Campbellite preacher,

[30]

Pointing a long finger at the Methodist preacher.
"And how could he be in without being immersed?"
Well, the Campbellite preacher won the debate.
But the next day Billy Bell,
An infidel we had here,
Met the Campbellite preacher and said:
"I suppose it wouldn't be possible for a man
To stand in water up to his knees
And have water sprinkled on his head, would it?"
And the Campbellite preacher said:
"Get thee behind me Satan," and went on.
Well Linkern was kind of an infidel,
And The Little Giant got caught in his own orthodoxy,
And his ability for debate led him into
The complete persuading of himself.
And by arguin' for the law
He made Linkern appear
As bein' against the law.

But just think, for a minute, young man:
Here is The Little Giant the greatest figure in all the
    land
And the wheel of fortune turns
And he stands by Linkern's side and holds
His hat while Linkern takes the oath
As president!
Then the war comes and his leadership
Has left him, and millions who followed him

Turn from him, and then Death comes,
And sits by him and says: Your time's up!
So I say when they put up that monument
And carved those words upon it
They had just as well have carved the words,
"He took poison."

Which reminds me:
There was a family over at Dutchland
Named Nitchie.
And my boy writes me from college
That there is a writer named Nitchie
Who says — well I can't tell you just now.
But if you'll look at things close
You'll see that Linkern was against the legal law,
And Douglas against the moral law so-called,
And neither cared for the other's law —
And that was the real debate!
Linkern rode over laws to save the Union,
And Douglas said he cared more for white supremacy
Than anything else.
Which being true, who can tell
Who won the debates?
Is it better to have the Union,
Or better to have a master race?

I'll go over to the post-office now
And see if there's a letter from my boy.

VII

AUTOCHTHON

In a rude country some four thousand miles
From Charles' and Alfred's birthplace you were born,
In the same year.   But Charles and you were born
On the same day, and Alfred six months later.
Thus start you in a sense the race together. . . .
Charles goes to Edinburgh, afterwards
His father picks him for the ministry,
And sends him off to Cambridge where he spends
His time on beetles and geology,
Neglects theology.   Alfred is here
Fondling a Virgil and a Horace.
But you — these years you give to reading Æsop,
The Bible, lives of Washington and Franklin,
And Kirkham's grammar.

In 1830 Alfred prints a book
Containing "Mariana," certain other
Delicate, wind-blown bells of airy music.
And in this year you move from Indiana
And settle near Decatur, Illinois,
Hard by the river Sangamon where fever
And ague burned and shook the poor
Swamp saffron creatures of that desolate land.
While Alfred walks the flowering lanes of England,

And reads Theocritus to the song of larks
You clear the forests, plow the stumpy land,
Fight off the torments of mosquitoes, flies
And study Kirkham's grammar.

In 1831 Charles takes a trip
Around the world, sees South America,
And studies living things in Galapagos,
Tahiti, Keeling Island and Tasmania.
In 1831 you take a trip
Upon a flat-boat down to New Orleans
Through hardships scarcely less than Joliet
And Marquette knew in 1673,
Return on foot to Orfutt's store at Salem.

By this time Jacques Rousseau was canonized;
Jefferson dead but seven years or so;
Brook Farm was budding, Garrison had started
His *Liberator*, Fourier still alive;
And Emerson was preening his slim wings
For flights into broad spaces — there was stir
Enough to sweep the Shelleyan heads, — in truth
Shelley was scarcely passed a decade then.
Old Godwin still was writing, wars for freedom
Swept through the Grecian Isles, America
Had "isms" in abundance, but not one
Took hold of you.

In 1832 Alfred has drawn

AUTOCHTHON

Out of old Mallory and Grecian myths
The "Lady of Shalott" and fair "Œnone,"
And put them into verse.
This is the year you fight the Black Hawk war,
And issue an address to Sangamon's people.
You are but twenty-three, yet this address
Would not shame Charles or Alfred; it's restrained,
And sanely balanced, without extra words,
Or youth's conceits, or imitative figures, dreams
Or "isms" of the day. No, here you hope
That enterprise, morality, sobriety
May be more general, and speak a word
For popular education, so that all
May have a "moderate education" as you say.
You make a plea for railroads and canals,
And ask the suffrages of the people, saying
You have known disappointment far too much
To be chagrined at failure, if you lose.
They take you at your word and send another
To represent them in the Legislature.
Then you decide to learn the blacksmith's trade.
But Fate comes by and plucks you by the sleeve,
And changes history, doubtless.

By '36 when Charles returns to England
You have become a legislator; yes
You tried again and won. You have become
A lawyer too, by working through the levels

Of laborer, store-keeper and surveyor,
Wrapped up in problems of geometry,
And Kirkham's grammar and Sir William Blackstone,
And Coke on Littleton, and Joseph Chitty.
Brook Farm will soon bloom forth, Francois Fourier
Is still on earth, and Garrison is shaking
Terrible lightning at Slavocracy.
And certain libertarians, *videlicet*
John Greenleaf Whittier and others, sing
The trampling out of grapes of wrath; in truth
The Hebrews taught the idealist how to sing
Destruction in the name of God and curse
Where strength was lacking for the sword — but you
Are not a Robert Emmet, or a Shelley,
Have no false dreams of dying to bring in
The day of Liberty.   At twenty-three
You're measuring the world and waiting for
Dawn's mists to clear that you may measure it,
And know the field's dimensions ere you put
Your handle to the plow.

In 1833 a man named Hallam,
A friend of Alfred's, died at twenty-two.
Thereafter Alfred worked his hopes and fears
Upon the dark impasto of this loss
In delicate colors.   And in 1850
When you were sunk in melancholia,
As one of no use in the world, adjudged

AUTOCHTHON

To be of no use by your time and place,
Alfred brought forth his Dante dream of life,
Received the laureate wreath and settled down
With a fair wife amid entrancing richness
Of sunny seas and silken sails and dreams
Of Araby,
And ivied halls, and meadows where the breeze
Of temperate England blows the hurrying cloud.
There, seated like an Oriental king
In silk and linen clothed took the acclaim
Of England and the world! . . .

                   This is the year
You sit in a little office there in Springfield,
Feet on the desk and brood. What are you thinking?
You're forty-one; around you spears are whacking
The wind-mills of the day, you watch and weigh.
The sun-light of your mind quivers about
The darkness every thinking soul must know,
And lights up hidden things behind the door,
And in dark corners. You have fathomed much,
Weighed life and men. O what a spheréd brain,
Strong nerved, fresh blooded, firm in plasmic fire,
And ready for a task, if there be one!
That is the question that makes brooding thought:
For you know well men come into the world
And find no task, and die, and are not known —
Great spheréd brains gone into dust again,
Their light under a bushel all their days!

THE GREAT VALLEY

In 1859, Charles publishes
His "Origin of Species," and 'tis said
You see it, or at least hear what it is.
Out of three travelers in a distant land
One writes a book of what the three have seen.
Perhaps you never read much, yet perhaps
Some books were just a record of your mind.
How had it helped you in your work to read
The "Idylls of the King"? As much, perhaps,
Had Alfred read the Northwest Ordinance
Of 1787. . . .

But in this year
Of '59 you're sunk in blackest thought
About the country maybe, but, I think,
About this riddle of our mortal life.
You were a poet, Abraham, from your birth.
That makes you think, and makes you deal at last
With things material to the tune of laws
Moving in higher spaces when you're called
To act — and show a poet moulding stuff
Too tough for spirits practical to mould.
Here are you with your feet upon the desk.
You have been beaten in a cause which kept
Some strings too loose to catch the vibrate waves
Of a great Harp whose music you have sensed.
You are a mathematician using symbols
Like Justice, Truth, with keenness to perceive

AUTOCHTHON

Disturbance of equations, a logician
Who sees invariable laws, and beauty born
Of finding out and following the laws.
You are a Plato brooding there in Springfield.
You are a poet with a voice for Truth,
And never to be claimed by visionaries
Who chant the theme of bread and bread alone.

                             But here and now
They want you not for Senator, it seems.
You have been tossed to one side by the rush
Of world events, left stranded and alone,
And fitted for no use, it seems, in Springfield.
A country lawyer with a solid logic,
And gift of prudent phrase which has a way
Of hardening under time to rock as hard
As the enduring thought you seal it with.
You've reached your fiftieth year, your occultation
Should pass.   If ever, we should see a light:
In all your life you have not seen a city.
But now our Springfield giant strides Broadway,
Thrills William Cullen Bryant, sets a wonder
Going about the East, that Kirkham's grammar
Can give a man such speech at Cooper Union,
Which even Alfred's, trained to Virgil's style,
Cannot disdain for matching in the thought
With faultless clearness.

And still in 1860 all the Brahmins
Have fear to give you power.
You are a backwoodsman, a country lawyer
Unlettered in the difficult art of states.
A denizen of a squalid western town,
Dowered with a knack of argument alone,
Which wakes the country school-house, and may lift
Its devotees to Congress by good fortune.
But then at Cooper Union intuitive eyes
Had measured your tall frame, and careful speech,
Your strength and self-possession.   Then they came
With that dramatic sense which is American
Into the hall with rails which you had split,
And called you Honest Abe, and wearing badges
With your face on them and the poor catch words
Of Honest Abe, as if you were a referee
Like Honest Kelly, when in truth no man
Had ever been your intimate, ever slapped you
With brisk familiarity, or called you
Anything but Mr. Lincoln, never
Abe, or Abraham, and never used
The Hello Bill of salutation to you —
O great patrician, therefore fit to be
Great democrat as well!

In 1862 Charles publishes
"How Orchid Flowers are Fertilized by Insects,"
And you give forth a proclamation saying

AUTOCHTHON

"The Union must have peace, or I wipe out
The blot of negro slavery. You see,
The symphony's the thing, and if you mar it,
Contending over slavery, I remove
The source of the disharmony. I admit
The freedom of the press — but for the Union.
When you abuse the Union, you shall stop.
And when you are in jail, no habeas corpus
Shall bring relief — I have suspended it."
To-day they call you libertarian —
Well, so you were, but just as Beauty is,
And Truth is, even if they curb and vanquish
The lower heights of beauty and of truth.
They take your speech and deeds and give you place
In Hebrew temples with Ezekiel,
Habakkuk and Isaiah — you emerge
From this association, master man!
You are not of the faith that breeds the ethic
Wranglers, who make economic goals
The strain and test of life. You are not one,
Spite of your lash and sword threat, who believe
God will avenge the weak. That is the dream
Which builds millenniums where disharmonies
That make the larger harmony shall cease —
A dream not yours. And they shall lose you who
Enthrone you as a prophet who cut through
The circle of our human sphere of life
To let in wrath and judgments, final tests

On Life around the price of sparrows, weights
Wherewith bread shall be weighed. . . . .

There is a windless flame where cries and tears,
Where hunger, strife, and war and human blood
No shadow cast, and where the love of Truth,
Which is not love of individual souls,
Finds solace in a Judgment of our life.
That is the Flame that took both Charles and You —
O leader in a Commonwealth of Thought!

VIII

GRANT AND LOGAN AND OUR TEARS

'Twixt certain parallels of latitude;
Say thirty-seven and forty-two and more;
And certain meridians, say ninety-one
And eighty-seven plus.
The top line drawn to leave the lower lake
Shaped like a drinking cup to meet your needs;
To bind you to the east and west,
Save you from tributary servitude
Through Mississippi's River to the south.
No sheds of hills to guard you on the north
Against the arctic winds loosed at the pole,
Or Medicine Hat parturient as the bag
Of Mad Æolus.
The valley and the river just a hall-way
Making a draft for tropic heat in summer —
Well, here you are in physiography.

Upon a time black soil was poured
Over your surface as the cook
Pours chocolate on a cake.
So you are fertile, never a land so rich.

A little river flowing in the lake
Vanishing in marshes up a mile or so
Makes for a portage to another stream

THE GREAT VALLEY

Which empties in another stream which empties
Into the Mississippi.
A spot between the lake and river lies
Upon the highway binding east and west,
And from the south and north where traders meet.
This is the very place to build a fort —
The fort becomes a town within a year,
A great metropolis in half a cycle.

Within a lifetime you have gained
Some seven million souls.
The land of Luther sends a swarming host;
And Milton's land adventurous sons;
And Scandinavia's realm,
And Michael Angelo's mountains,
All Europe pours her wealth
Of brawn and spirit on you,
Until you are an empire
Of restless vital men, and teeming towns.

Before you were grown rich,
And populous
You brightened history;
Great men came from you.
But now that you have cities and great treasure
Where are your great ones?
What is your genius?
What star enwraps your eyes?

GRANT AND LOGAN AND OUR TEARS

What heights allure you?
Hermaphroditic giant, sad and drunk
Not gay, but foolish, stuffed with new baked bread,
Who took away your gland pituitary,
Abandoned you to such exaggerate growth
Without increase of soul?
You blasphemous, yet afraid,
Licentious, yet ashamed,
Swaggering, yet blubbering
And boasting of your rights.
Materialist who woos the spiritual,
Who holds aloft the cross from which you've sold
The nails to junk-men.
And makes a hackle from the crown of thorns
Wherewith to hackle hemp to make a rope
For your own hanging in the Philippines!
Who with one hand grabs off the widow's mite,
And with the other tosses golden coins
Into the beggar's cup.
The black-snake whip in one hand, in the other
A plentiful supply of surgeon's tape.   Oh you!
A hard oppressor, charitably inclined,
And keen to see and take the outward image —
Devoid of categories to reduce
Its truth and meaning.

No seed of old world thistles should be sown here,
Or let to fly upon this soil.

Yet dogma has been sown here
Men rise thereby who sow the seed again;
Accessory spirits keep the ground well stirred.
It's gold and then it's power, but gold at last.
And for the rest what are your dominant breeds?
Smug cultures where the aggregate mind is leather
Gorged with the oil respectability
Impervious to thought.
These pick the eunuch type as being safe,
American, it's called:
Sleek, quiet, smiling, ready servitors
Who for the salary, and that alone,
(Require no bribes)
Effect the business will.

You are a hollow thing of steel, a cauldron,
No monument of freedom.
You're lettered, it is true,
With many luminous truths that came to be
Through deeds of men who died for liberty.
But inside you there is a seething compost
Of public schools, the ballot, journalism,
Laws, jurisprudence, dogma, gold the chief
Ingredient all stirred into a brew
Wherewith to feed yourself and keep yourself
The thing you are!
Not wholly slave, not really free,
Desiring vaguely to be master moral,

GRANT AND LOGAN AND OUR TEARS

And yet too sicklied over by old truths,
The ballot, fear, plebian spirit, lack of mind,
To reach patrician levels —
Hermaphroditic giant, misty-eyed,
Half blinded by ideals, half by greed!

Can nothing but a war,
The prospect of a slaughter or the prize
Of foreign lands, shake off your lethargy,
And make you seem as big in spirit as
You are in body?
Would you not love the general weal improved?
Would you not love your towns made beautiful?
Your halls and courts
Reclaimed from dicers' oaths?
Your laws made just and tuned to god-like laws?
Your weights and measures made invariable?
Is there no tonic in such hopes as these
To rouse you, giant?

I think you are Delilah
Tricked out as Liberty for a fancy ball,
Spiritless, provincal, shabby, dull,
Where no ways gentle, no natural mirth prevails.
You've put your Samson's eye out; he would see.
You've chained him to the grinder, he would play,
Be wise and human, free, courageous, fair,
Of cleaner flesh and nobler spirit. Look

He may pull down your bastard temple yet,
And make you use pentelic marble for
Rebuilding of the Parthenon you planned,
And leave the misse stone thrown in a heap
For sheep gates in the walls of Ancient Zion!

THE MUNICIPAL PIER

Great snail whose lofty horns are knobbed with gold;
Long javelin of red-wood lying straight
Upon the changing indigos which unfold
In blues and chrysophrases from the gate
Of this our city sea-ward, till the gull
Becomes a gnat where lights annihilate
The wings' last beat! Or are you like a hull
Pompeiian red upon the Nile's slate green?
Or are you like these clouds which fanciful
Half open eyes make giant fish serene,
And motionless as rifts of carbuncles
Sunk in a waste of faience sky, between
Such terrifying turquoise? Darkness dulls
The torches of your towers struck to flame
By sun-set, and you mass amid the hulls
Of shadows on the water, then reclaim
This blackness with a thousand eyes of light!
Peiræus made with hands, which over-came
The waters, where no point of land gave might
To walls and slips, no Peiraic promontory
Inspired our Hippodamus in his flight
Sea-ward with docks, parades, an auditory

THE GREAT VALLEY

For music and a dancing floor for youths,
But only the sea tempted. Telling the story
That grows within the loop, its dens and booths,
And palaces of trade, is to omit
The city's lofty genius and the truths
Through which she works at best, against the wit
Of creatures who would sell her body, take
The money of the sale as perquisite
For grossness in luxurious life. Awake
Themistocles of us and carve the dream
Of Burnham into stone! Along this lake
Such as no city looks on, to redeem
Its shores from shrieks and crashes, refuse, smoke
His architectural vision sketched the scheme
Of harbors, islands, boulevards — he spoke
For these, the concourse, stadium and a tomb
For that dull infamy of filth whose cloak
Is law, hiding the greedy hands that doom
To long delay with bribery. He is gone
These several years into the narrow room
Where beauty is no more of walk or lawn,
Or arch or peristyle, but still he says:
"Work quickly into form what I have drawn,
And give Chicago of these middle days
The glory which it merits: To this Pier
Make wide the marble way, build new the quays
Give to the swimmers depths made fresh and clear,
Lay out the flowering gardens, founts and pools

THE MUNICIPAL PIER

Such as Versailles knows.   The river steer
Under the arches of two decked bascules."
Look at the photographs of seventy-six,
Whoever you are who mocks or ridicules
This city, then imagine stones and bricks
Which from such lowness rose, in fifty years
By so much grown miraculous to transfix
The future's wonder as ours is for piers
Like this, Chicago!   O ye men who wield
Small strength or great or none, too apt at sneers
For men who did too little, you must yield
Your names for judgment soon, have you done more
To make this city great than Marshall Field?
While you were railing, idling, on this shore
Hands silent, out of sight were plunged in toil.
You woke one morning to the waters' roar
And saw these gilded turrets flash and spoil
The sun-light of the spring.   What have you sown
Of truth or beauty in this eager soil
To make your living felt, your labor known?
Sometimes I see silk banners in the sky,
And hear the sound of silver trumpets blown,
And bells high turreted.   And passing by
This firmament of rolling blue great throngs
Stream in an air of brilliant sun where I
A century gone am of it, when my songs
Are but a record of a day that died,
And saw the end of desecrating wrongs.

THE GREAT VALLEY

How sweet bells are borne on the evening tide
High up where heaven is flushed and the moon's
    sphere
Looks down on temples, arches, where the wide
Eternal waters thunder round the Pier!

GOBINEAU TO TREE

Since our talk at Christiana I have read
All you referred me to concerning Lincoln:
His speeches and the story of the struggle
Which ended in your war, not civil really
But waged between two nations — but no matter!
To me whose life is closing, and whose life
Was spent in struggle, much of misery,
In friendship with De Tocqueville then at odds
With him and his philosophy, who knew
Bismarck, who saw the wars of Europe, saw
Great men come up and fall, and systems change,
Who probed into the Renaissance and mastered
Religions and philosophies and wrote
Concerning racial inequalities —
To me I say this crisis of your time
And country seems remote as it might be
Almost in far Australia, trivial
In substance and effect, or world result.
And now your letter and these documents
Concerning Douglas yield but scanty gold.
Perhaps I've reached an age where I cannot
Digest new matter, or resolve its worth,
Extract its bearing and significance.

THE GREAT VALLEY

But since you ask me I am writing you
What I've arrived at.

                         From the photographs
And the descriptions of your Illinois,
Where Lincoln spent his youth, I almost sicken:
Small muddy rivers flanked by bottom lands
So fat of fertile stuff the grossest weeds
Thrive thriftier than in Egypt, round their roots
Repulsive serpents crawl, the air is full
Of loathsome insects, and along these banks
An agued people live who have no life
Except hard toil, whose pleasures are the dance
Where violent liquor takes the gun or knife;
Who have no inspiration save the orgy
Of the religious meeting, where the cult
Of savage dreams is almost theirs.   The towns
Places of filth, of maddening quietude;
Streets mired with mud, board sidewalks where the men,
Like chickens with the cholera, stand and squeak
Foul or half-idiot things; near by the churches,
Mere arch-ways to the grave-yard.   Nothing here
Of conscious plan to lift the spirit up.
All is defeat of liberty in spite
Of certain strong men, certain splendid breeds,
The pioneers who made your state; no beauty
Save as a soul delves in a master book.
And out of this your Lincoln came, not poor

GOBINEAU TO TREE

As Burns was in a land of storied towers,
But poor as a degenerate breed is poor
Sunk down in squalor.

                  Yet he seems a man
Of master qualities.   The muddy streets,
And melancholy of a pastoral town,
And sights of people sick, the stifling weeds
Which grew about him left his spirit clean,
Save for an ache that all his youth was spent
In such surroundings.

                And observe the man!
Do poverty and life among such people
Make him a libertarian?   Let us see.
At twenty years he is a centralist,
Stands for the bank which Andrew Jackson fought,
And lauds protection, thinks of Washington
Much more than Springfield.   That is right I say —
But call him not a democrat.

                    Look here!
This master book of Stephens which you sent me
Accuses Lincoln of imperial deeds,
And breach of laws, and rightly so, in truth.
That makes me love him, but the end he sought
Is something else.   At first that was the Union,
Straight through it was the Union, but at last

[55]

The strain of Christian softness always his
Which filled him full of hate for slavery
Cropped out in freedom for your negro slaves,
Which was an act of war, and so confessed,
Not propped by law, but only by a will.
Thus he became a man who broke all law
To have his law.   He killed a million men
For what he called the Union, what he thought
Was truth of Christian brotherhood.   I say
He killed a million men, for it is true
Your war had never come, had he believed
All government must rest in men's consent.
What have we but a soul imperial?
A brother to me, standing for the strong,
For master races, blindly at the work
Of biologic mount?   The cells of him
That make him saint for radicals and dreamers
Are but somatic, but the sperm of him
Will propagate great rulers.

                              See his face!
Its tragic pathos fools the idealist —
But study it.   First, then, observe the eyes,
And tell me how within their gaze events
Or men could lose their true proportions!   Here
No visions swarm, no dreams with flashing wings
Throw light upon them.   No, they only look
Across a boundless prairie, that is all.

GOBINEAU TO TREE

And in that brow and nose we see a strength
Slow, steady, wary, cautious — why this man
Is your conservative, perhaps your best,
Which is one reason why he loved the Union,
And even said at last that government
Of the people meant the Union — how absurd ! —
Would perish, if it perished, clearly false !
And if 'twere true would be the better.   Read
My Renaissance, and other books, you'll see
How I'd protect the master spirits, keep
The master races pure ; how I detest
The brotherhood of man, how I have shown
The falseness of these Galilean dreams,
These syrups strained in secret, used to drug
The strong and make them equal with the weak.
Such things are of the mind which weaves in space, —
A penalty of thought.   Come back to earth,
Live close to nature.   Do not sap a rose
To nourish cabbages, and call it truth !

Well, then, your negro's freed !   But what of that ?
You do not want him for a friend or spouse.
I would not see him whipped, or made a bond.
But tell me what you're thinking of who say
His freedom is a gain for liberty ?
To buy men's labor is to buy their bodies.
Your country now has entered on a course
Of buying labor, wait and see what comes !

THE GREAT VALLEY

I see processions filing through your land.
They carry banners bearing Lincoln's face.
And there are hordes who think the kingdom's coming:
As Lincoln freed the slaves, one will arise
To free all men! The signs before the war
Are come again, portentous stars appear
Which prophesied the war! All revolutions
Are so announced, the world is rising higher
Through ordered revolutions, preordained!
Well, certain men look at these mad processions
From well-protected windows, with a smile —
They are your millionaires, they think they know
The soul of Lincoln better than the crowds
That carry banners with his picture on them.
Yes, all they have they owe to Lincoln, they
Grew strong through Lincoln.

                    But are you content
To have your negroes free, and millionaires
In mastership of your republic? Where
Are men to overlord your millionaires? You know
Out of the eater comes forth meat, who will
Exhaust the strength of those whose strength was gained
From blood of boys shed on the battle field?
What can you do to have a Renaissance
That with a terrible light will drive to covert
Owls, bats, and mousing hawks, that neither know
What life is, whence they come, nor what they are,

GOBINEAU TO TREE

Who live by superstition, codes of slaves,
Fear truth, are weak, and only hunger know —
You must have such a Renaissance or die
While slipping smugly, self sufficiently
Along a way unvisioned, while you play
The hypocrite as it was never played
In any place, in any time on earth!
These things I see.   But let me in conclusion
Point to your Lincoln as a man who makes
For power and beauty in your country, call it
Republic if you will, the name is nothing.
I say the vitalest force is love, not hate.
I say that all great souls are lovers, but of what?
Why, what great Goethe loved!   Your master men
Should learn of Goethe, hold the crowd through him.
And Lincoln was a lover, but of what?
Well not the cesspool of the black man's slavery.
He loved the mathematics of high truths,
And heightened spirituality, that's the reason
Only a man like me can know him, that's
The reason that your crude American thought
Misses the man.

OLD PIERY

I had a paying little refinery
And all was well with me, and then
The Trust edged up to me and wiped me out.
So much for northern tariff, freedom
Of niggers and New England rule.
Praise God for sponging slavery from the Slate!
Well, then I was without a cent again,
What should I do?   I wanted first a change,
And rest in the use of other faculties,
So I went out and took a farm.   '
One thing leads to another.   I wake up one morning
And find a man from Illinois
Become my neighbor on the adjoining farm.
It's your John Cogdall, once of Petersburg,
County of Menard, in Illinois,
Precinct Indian Point, he said to me.
We're friends at once, and visit back and forth.
Two months ago I saw upon his table
A copy of the *Petersburg Observer* —
John likes to hear the home-town news —
I pick it up and scan it through to see
What a country paper is in Illinois.

OLD PIERY

And there I read this notice of "Old Piery,"
Real name Cordelia Stacke, dead thirty years,
Whose money in the county treasury
Is to be made escheat.   So here I am
Maneuvering for this money, rather shabby
If I was not so devilish poor and pressed;
If letting Menard County have the prize
Would profit any one, when I can prove
Old Piery was my great aunt,
Her father and my grandfather brothers,
When I can prove that I'm her only heir.

Yes, but not as pure of blood.
Her father was a judge in South Carolina,
Her mother was a belle of New Orleans,
My father told me so.   Cordelia Stacke,
"Old Piery," as you called her, was a story
We heard as children sitting on his knee.
I know to prove my name is Stacke,
And then because her name was Stacke
Won't draw this money from your treasury,
But wait
Go to your vault and get that ring she wore,
Slipped from her dead hand when you found her body
Dead for a week amid her rags and stuff.
Go get that ring, Mr. Treasurer of Menard,
If I don't describe it
Down to the finest point,

THE GREAT VALLEY

Just as I heard my father say
The night she disappeared she wore a ring
Of such and such, I'll go back to my farm
In Mississippi.   But I'll do much more
I'll trace her from Columbia to Old Salem;
I'll show her crazed brain luring her along
To find the spot where Lincoln kept the store
Two miles from where we sit.
She must have walked
Across Virginia, West Virginia,
Ohio, Indiana, or perhaps
She footed it through Tennessee, Kentucky.

I talked this morning with your county judge.
He said she came here late in '65
Or early '66,
Was seen by farmers near the Salem Mill,
A loitering, mumbling woman,
Not old, but looking old, and aging fast
As she became a figure in your streets
And alleys with a gunny-sack on back,
Wherein she stuffed old bottles, paper, things
She picked industriously and stored away.
Would buy a bit of cold food at the baker's.
Sometimes would sit on door steps eating cake,
Which friendly hands had given her, then depart
And say, "God rest your souls!"   Attended mass
On Sunday mornings, knew no one

OLD PIERY

And had no friends.
In '69 was found incompetent,
And placed in charge of a conservator.
Then as she was not dangerous went ahead
At picking rags,
Until in '97 passed away.

Such was the life and death of a fine girl,
The daughter of a judge in South Carolina
And a belle of New Orleans.
And after life at best knew life at worst,
Beginning in a southern capitol
Where she knew riches, admiration, place,
She ended up in Petersburg, Illinois,
A little croaking, mad but harmless waif,
A withered leaf stirred by the Lincoln storm.
And here's my guess:
The fancy of her madness brought her here
To see the country where
The man who was a laborer, kept a store,
Could rise therefrom,
And bring such desolation to the South,
Such sorrow to herself, that is my guess.

The name's Cordelia Stacke inside this ring
You tell me.   She's the same no doubt.
We all lived in Columbia when the troops
Of Sherman whirled upon us to the sea.

I was a year old then.   We were burned out,
Lost everything.
The troops came howling, plundering,
And tossing combustible chemicals.
They butchered just for sport our cattle;
Split chests and cabinets with savage axes;
Walked with their hob-nailed boots on our pianos;
Ran bayonets through pictures;
Rode horses in our parlors;
Broke open trunks and safes;
Searched cellars, opened graves for hoarded gold,
And yelled "You dirty rebels now we've got you."
They filled their bellies up with wine and whisky,
And drunken, howling through Columbia's streets
They carried vases, goblets, silver, gold,
And rolled about with pockets full of loot,
And then at last they stuck the torch to us
And made a bon-fire of our city.

Cordelia had a lover who was killed
At Antietam fighting, not for niggers,
But fighting back the fools who had been crazed
By preachers, poets, Garrisons and Whittiers
Who thought they worked for freedom, but instead
Worked for New England's tariff — look at me
How could the trust destroy me if the tariff
Put no bricks in the bully's boxing gloves?
Well, then, Cordelia lost her lover,

OLD PIERY

And when the troops came was a novitiate
Nun at the convent.   And the soldiers came
To say the convent would be spared.   But when
The flames arose, she ran into the city
To be beside her father and her mother.
And she arrived
Just as the soldiers entered the house for loot.
Her mother was in bed half dead from fright,
Not well at best.
The soldiers broke the bedroom door,
And howled for treasure.   When the mother said
There was no treasure, then they took her
And flung her from the bed, ripped up the matress,
Raked pictures from the walls, and smashed the mirrors,
Tore closets open, then went to the cellar
Leaving the mother lying on the floor,
Who lay as dead.
They drank what wine they found,
Then seized the father, hung him to a tree
To make him tell where he kept money hidden.
The mother died in two days from the fright.
The father was not killed, they took him down,
And went their way carousing, yelling out
"You dirty rebels now we've got you fair."
Cordelia thought no doubt that both were dead.
A passerby beheld her on the lawn
Her hair let down and plucking at her dress.
But who could stop to help her in that hell

Of a city burning and the howls and shouts,
And falling walls?
Cordelia disappeared and from that night
Was never seen or heard of.   To his death
Her father thought she met a terrible fate:
Was raped and slaughtered.

                              So you see
All of this put together tells the story
Of this poor creature whom you called "Old Piery."
But let me add Cordelia had a horse
She called "Old Piery" — that fits in my proof.
That's why she named herself "Old Piery" here,
And gave your boys and girls a mocking name
To hail her with as she went up your alleys;
With which to rap the windows of her room,
Where bottles, cans, waste rags, and copper things,
Old hoops of iron, staves, old boots and shoes,
Springs, wheels of clocks, and locks of broken guns,
Old boards and boxes, stacks of paper waste
Stuffed up the place, and where unknown to all
Paper and silver money hid in cracks
Between the leaves of fouled and rain-soaked books,
Or packed in jars were kept by her.   You see
Her mind was turned to treasure, hiding it
Against the soldiers maybe, in this land
Where Lincoln was a laborer, farmer, kept
A store at Salem.

OLD PIERY

                    Well I say
God rest her soul, as she was used to say.
I want to raise a stone to mark her grave,
And carve her name below a broken heart.
For listen now: the ring Cordelia wore
Was just a little band of gold and set
With a cornelian heart — am I not right?
I knew I was.

THE TYPICAL AMERICAN?

He calls himself an American citizen —
And yet among such various breeds of men
Who'll call him typical?   At any rate
His faults or virtues one may predicate
Somewhat as follows : He is sent to school
Little or much, where he imbibes the rule
Of safety first and comfort; in his youth
He joins the church and ends the quest of truth.
Beyond the pages of theology
He does not turn, he does not seem to see
How hunger makes these Occidental creeds
Sweet foliage on which the stomach feeds.
Like those thick tussock moths upon the bole
Of a great beech tree, feed the human soul
And it will use the food for gold and power!
So men have used Christ Jesus' tender flower,
And garnered it for porridge, opiates,
And made it flesh of customs laws and states
Where life repeats itself after a plan
And breeds the typical American —
As he regards himself.

                Our man matures
And enters business, following the lures

THE TYPICAL AMERICAN?

Of great increase in business, more receipts —
Upon this object center all his wits.
And greater crops make needful larger barns,
Vainly the parable of Jesus warns.
His soul is now required, is taken away
From living waters, in a little day
Thrift, labor dooms him, leaves him banqueting
Where nothing nourishes, they are the sting
Which deadens him and casts him down at last
Fly blown or numb or lifeless in this vast
Surrounding air of Vital Power, where God
Like the great sun, invites the wayside clod
To live at full.

              In time our hero weds
A woman like himself, and little heads
Soon run about a house or pleasant yard.
He must work now to keep them — have regard
To the community, its thoughts and ways.
What church is here?   He finds it best to praise
Its pastor and its flock, his children send
To Sunday school, if never he attend
Its services.   What politics obtain?
He must support the tussock leaf campaigns
If he would eat himself.   'Tis best to join
The party which controls the greater coin.
And so what is his party's interest
In business?   There must his soul invest

THE GREAT VALLEY

Its treasure till the two are wholly one.
Like the poor prostitute he is undone
In virtue not alone, but he has made
Himself a cog-wheel in the filthy trade
Of justice courts, police and graft in wine
Bondsmen and lawyers with a strength malign
Moving the silken vestured marionette
To laugh, entice and play the sad coquette.
Yet if for bread you are compelled to ask
The giver may impose an evil task,
Or terms of life.   Would you retain a roof,
Mix with the crowd, nor dare to stand aloof.
Our hero sees this, wears a hopeful smile
To cover up his spattered soul, and while
Digesting wounded truth, hiding his thought,
His own opinions, for his soul is caught
Amid the idiot hands that strike and press —
One may glide through who learns to say yes, yes,
While in heart-sickness whispering to himself:
I do this for the children, and for pelf
To keep the house and yard, the cupboard full.
Some time I hope to free myself and pull
My legs out of this social muck and mire.
First money is, then freedom his desire,
But often neither comes.   If he win wealth
He has become lead-poisoned, for by stealth
The virus of the colors which he used
To paint his life is spread and interfused

THE TYPICAL AMERICAN?

In every vein.   By ways complaisant
Our hero has got gold from ignorant
Vulgarian nondescripts, has entertained
The odorous cormorants, and has profaned
His household gods to keep them safe and whole
Upon the altar — winning what a goal!
For meantime in this living he has schooled
His children in the precepts which have ruled
His days from the beginning.   They are bred
His out-look to repeat, and even to tread
The way he went amid the tangled wood
In their own time and chosen neighborhood.
What has our hero done?   Why nothing more
Than feed upon the beech leaves, gather store
For children moths to feed on, and get strength
To climb the branches and on leaves at length
To feed of their own will.

                    Is this a man?
Is this your typical American?

COME, REPUBLIC

Come! United States of America,
And you one hundred million souls, O Republic,
Throw out your chests, lift up your heads,
And walk with a soldier's stride.
Quit burning up for money alone.
Quit slouching and dawdling,
And dreaming and moralising.
Quit idling about the streets, like the boy
In the village, who pines for the city.
Root out the sinister secret societies,
And the clans that stick together for office,
And the good men who care nothing for liberty,
But would run you, O Republic, as a household is run.
It is time, Republic, to get some class,
It is time to harden your muscles,
And to clear your eyes in the cold water of Reality,
And to tighten your nerves.
It is time to think what Nature means,
And to consult Nature,
When your soul, as you call it, calls to you
To follow principle!
It is time to snuff out the A. D. Bloods.

COME, REPUBLIC

It is time to lift yourself, O Republic,
From the street corners of Spoon River.

Do you wish to survive,
And to count in the years to come?
Then do what the plow-boys did in sixty-one,
Who left the fields for the camp,
And tightened their nerves and hardened their arms
Till the day they left the camp for the fields
The bravest, readiest, clearest-eyed
Straight-walking men in the world,
And symbolical of a Republic
That is worthy the name!

If you, Republic, had kept the faith
Of a culture all your own,
And a spiritual independence,
And a freedom large and new.
If you had not set up a Federal judge in China,
And scrambled for place in the Orient,
And stolen the Philippine Islands,
And mixed in the business of Europe,
Three thousand miles of water east,
And seven thousand west
Had kept your hands untainted, free
For a culture all your own!
But while you were fumbling, and while you were
    dreaming

As the boy in the village dreams of the city
You were doing something worse:
You were imitating!
You came to the city and aped the swells,
And tried to enter their set!
You strained your Fate to their fate,
And borrowed the mood to live their life!
And here you are in the game, Republic,
But not prepared to play!

But you did it.
And the water east and water west
Are no longer your safeguard:
They are now your danger and difficulty!
And you must live the life you started to imitate
In spite of these perilous waters.
For they keep you now from being neutral —
For you are not neutral, Republic,
You only pretend to be.
You are not free, independent, brave,
You are shackled, cowardly
For what could happen to you overnight
In the Orient,
If you stood with your shoulders up,
And were Neutral!

Suppose you do it, Republic.
Get some class,

COME, REPUBLIC

Throw out your chest, lift up your head,
Be a ruler in the world,
And not a hermit in regimentals with a flint-lock.
Colossus with one foot in Europe,
And one in China,
Quit looking between your legs for the re-appearance
Of the star of Bethlehem —
Stand up and be a man!

PAST AND PRESENT

Past midnight!   Vastly overhead
A wash of stars — the town's asleep!
And through the pine trees of the dead
The rising winds of morning creep.

Dim, mid the hillside's shadow grass
I count the marble slabs.   How vain
My throbbing life that waits to pass
Into the great world on the train!

The city's vision fades from mind.
I only see the hill and sky;
And on the mist that rides the wind
A tottering pageant meets my eye.

The cock crows faintly, far away;
A troop of age and grief appears.
Ye shadows of a distant day.
What do ye, pioneers?

There shines the engine's comet light.
Ye shadows of a century set,
Haste to the hillside and the night —
I am not of you yet!

ROBERT G. INGERSOLL

To the lovers of Liberty everywhere,
But chiefly to the youth of America
Who did not know Robert G. Ingersoll,
Remember that he helped to make you free!
He was a leader in a war of guns for freedom,
But a general in the war of ideas for freedom!
He braved the misunderstanding of friends,
He faced the enmity of the powerful small of soul,
And the insidious power of the churches;
He put aside worldly honours,
And the sovereignty of place,
He stripped off the armor of institutional friendships
To dedicate his soul
To the terrible deities of Truth and Beauty! ?
And he went down into age and into the shadow
With love of men for a staff,
And the light of his soul for a light —
And with these alone!
O you martyrs trading martyrdom for heaven,
And self-denial for eternal riches,
How does your work and your death compare
With a man's for whom the weal of the race,
And the cause of humanity here and now were enough
To give life meaning and death as well? —
I have not seen such faith in Israel!

AT HAVANA

I met a fisherman at Havana once,
Havana on the Illinois, I mean,
There by the house and fish boats. He was burned
The color of an acorn, and his hair
Was coarse as a horse's tail. His scraggy hands
Looked like thick bands of weather-colored copper,
But his eyes were blue as faded gingham is.
I stood amid the smell of scales and heads,
And fishes' entrails dumped along the sand.
The still air was a burning glass which focused
A bon-fire sun right through my leghorn hat;
And a black fly from crannies of the air
Lit on my hand and bit it venomously.
Across the yellow river lay the bottoms
Where giant sycamores and elms o'ertopped
A jungle of disgusting weeds. The breeze
Hot as a tropic breath exhaled the reek
Of baking mud and of those noisome weeds,
Wherewith the odors of putrescent fish
Mixed on the simmering sands. A naturalist
Must seek the habitat of the life he studies. . . .
There on a platform lay the dressed fish, carp,
Black-bass, and pike and pickerel, buffalo,

AT HAVANA

Cat-fish, which I had come to see, and talk
With fishermen along the Illinois.
My man held up a fish and said to me;
"Here is the bastard who drives all the fish
Out of the river, out of any water
He comes in, and he comes wherever food
Can be obtained; the black-bass, even cat-fish,
And all the good stocks run away from him,
He is so hoggish, plaguy, and so mean.
The other fish may try to live with him,
I'm thinking sometimes, anyway I know
He drives the others out." I looked to see
What fish is so unfriendly to his fellows.
"Just look at him," he said, but as he spoke
The black fly stung my hand again. When I
Looked up from swatting him, the man had thrown
The fish upon the sand, and a stray dog
Was running off with him along the river.

THE MOURNER'S BENCH

They're holding a revival at New Hope Meeting house,
I can't keep from going, I ought to stay away.
For I come home and toss in bed till day,
· For thinking of my sin, and the trouble I am in.
I dream I hear the dancers
In the steps and swings,
The quadrilles and the lancers
They danced at Revis Springs.
I lie and think of Charley, Charley, Charley
The Bobtown dandy
Who had his way with me.
And no one is so handy
A dancer as Charley
To Little Drops of Brandy,
Or the Wind that Shakes the Barley,
Or Good mornin' Uncle Johnny I've fetched your
    Wagon Home.

And Greenberry Atterberry, who toed it like a pigeon
Has gone and got religion;
He's deserted the dancers, the fiddlers, merry-makers,
And I should do it too.
For Charley, Charley has left me for to roam.

THE MOURNER'S BENCH

But a woman at the mourner's bench must tell her story
    true —
What shall I do? What shall I do?

My grandmother told me of Old Peter Cartwright
Who preached hell-fire
And the worm that never dies.
And here's a young preacher at the New Hope Meeting
    house,
And every one allows, he has old Peter's brows,
And flaming of the eyes,
And the very same way, they say.
Last night he stuck his finger right down in my direc-
    tion,
And said: "God doesn't care
For your woman's hair.
Jesus wants to know if your soul is fair
As your woman's complexion."
And then I thought he knew —
O what shall I do?

Greenberry Atterberry, weeping and unsteady
Had left his seat already.
He stood at the mourner's bench in great tribulation
And told the congregation:
That fiddling and dancing and tobacco chewin'
Led up to whisky and to woman's ruin —
And I thought he looked at me.

G   [81]

Well, you can stop dancing, and you can stop drinking
And you can leave the quarter-horses at the crooked
    races.
But a woman, a woman, the people will be thinking
Forever of a woman who confesses her behavior.
And then I couldn't look in the people's faces,
All weeping and singing, O gentle Saviour!
Then the devil said: You wench
You'd cut a pretty figure at the mourner's bench,
Go out and look for Charley,
Go out and look for Charley,
He's down at Leese's Grove.
He has found a fresh love
Go win him back again.
He is dancing on the platform to the Speckled Hen.

O Saviour, Saviour, how can I join the mourners,
Face all the scorners?
But how can I hunt Charley at Leese's Grove?
How can I stand the staring, the whispering of things
Down at Revis Springs?
How can I stand the mocking of the fiddle strings?
Charley! Charley!
So it's knowing what's best to do,
Saviour! Saviour!
Its knowing what's best to do!

THE BAY-WINDOW

She sat at a bay-window where she saw
First open carriages and buggies pass!
And then Victorias with horses docked
And bits and buckles, chains of shining brass.
And then the horseless carriage, till at last
The swallow-gleam of varnished limousines
Silent as shadows took her lifted eye,
Uplifted from a book.   She always sat
In her bay-window with a book,
And with a tinted fan in summer-time.

But first she was a bride
Before the war.
Springing from honest blood, her place
Passed over lightly as her grandeur grew:
She was of seed too vital to decay
Wholly in any soil, the sort that grows and blooms
Where never gardener comes.
And this bay-window!   An aging man of gold
Had plucked her up, and here she rests and breathes
The free air of Chicago's reclamation.
And then she is
A wonder-bride for her brown hair,

THE GREAT VALLEY

And gray-blue eyes, and laughter, sunny wit,
And naturally patrician ways and speech,
(Acquiring French now that the chance has come),
And she is eighteen and is born to rule.

And her great merchant husband with blue eyes,
And strong beaked English nose,
Walks straighter for a pride that she is his.
Gives her a country place spaced out in walks,
And flower beds, where now such flimsy flats
Confront Grand Boulevard!
And for a city house he builds a house
Three stories high at Twentieth street,
Where then the manifest was sand and oaks,
And what is now the Loop, was just as far
As Hyde Park from the Loop is now.

In this bay-window then she sits a bride,
And sees the scrub oak cut and mansions fill
Gradually year by year the waste of sand.
For fashion follows her and builds beside her,
Till Prairie Avenue becomes the street
Of millionaires, who hear from traveled wives
What London is, what Paris is,
And open purses to unfolding tastes
For canvases and sculpture.
For every one grows rich now in Chicago.
And in the seventies women go to Paris,

THE BAY-WINDOW

Herself among the first, at least the chief,
See Egypt and see Rome.
And when returned drive down where wondering eyes
Along the marble terrace promenading,
Where Michigan Avenue was bounded by
The Lake across the street,
Behold the striped silk of their parasols
Fluttering over plumes and dancing eyes,
And purple velvet of Victorias.

For now it is the classic age!
There is the driving park,
There is the Palmer House,
There are cathedrals too.
There are the lofty ceilings walnut trimmed,
And foliate chandeliers of polished brass,
And marble-slabbed buffets with heavy cupids,
And clustered fruits carved in their sombre wood,
And square pianos with their rosewood legs
Swelled out with oval figures like great plums.
And paintings deeply daubed in brown asphaltum
Where chiaroscuro ends were lost in shadows,
Not lost in light, depressionistic things,
From which her lambent intuition led her.
She was among the first to catch the psychic
Waves that sweep around this little world
And change all things.
She traveled much and lived in Europe much,

THE GREAT VALLEY

Returning to her window where she watched
The city pass and bow its admiration,
The half of whom she knew as time went on,
Though all knew her and said "there is the queen,"
Or "there she is who thinks she is the queen."

And when the opera came she was the queen,
At least a queen whose sovereignty withstood
Encroaching claims to ripen into rights.
But then if all were lost where not a million
People lived as yet, and where, oh well
Packers and others threw their heavier gold
In what was once a scale of primogeniture,
Rome stood and London stood and Paris.
Have your own way at home, the mood began,
I am off here where you can scarcely come.
The next place is the best, a far off place
Has teasing witcheries to those at home.
Her husband now was dead some years, the children
Grown up, or off to school, a daughter married
To an Italian count kept state in Florence
Where Browning came, with whom our queen would
        fence
In spiritual dialectics.   In her travels
She had known Ibsen, Patti and George Eliot,
Sat as a dinner guest by Beaconsfield,
And taken tea upon Hawarden's lawn.
And so in escritoires and cabinets

THE BAY-WINDOW

She kept mementoes of her days abroad :
Like letters from George Eliot,
"Ferishtah's Fancies" inscribed by Robert.
And in the course of time this three-floored house
Was filled with treasures, tapestries,
Etruscan things, and faience peacock blue,
And oriental jade with letters of gold.
And there she reigned, but lived alone
The house kept by French maids
And impeccable butlers.
And so the years went, and she saw at last
The city start to slip away from her
And make her royal isolation
An ignorant solitude !

Yet she was beautiful at forty years,
Some years a widow then and very rich.
She was most fresh and matronly at fifty.
At fifty-five and sixty she could charm
A man of any age.   And master-men
Paid suit to her and gained
The stimulating richness of her mind.
Some said they did not want her, others said
Her wisdom and self-mastery froze their hearts.
But when she spoke she said she could not change
The name she loved, or change her place in life
To forced forgetfulness of that English face,
Who lifted up her life from some obscurity

And made it flower.
At any rate she lived for forty years
With only maids and butlers in a house
Round which the warring city crept,
Until at last the street with lowered pulse
Saw vacant mansions, as the mob psychology,
Which sways in fashion, brought an exodus.
But she knew no temptation to depart.
This was her house, her center of the world.
And when the Countess left the Count she came
To ease her mother's loneliness — oh yes!
Six months of loneliness was quite enough.
And then in spite of everything she left,
Returned to Florence and her rascal count,
Because she could not stand the loneliness,
And saw ahead long years of loneliness
In some bay window — no, it could not be!
And so she left her mother sitting there
Now sixty-eight or so,
Who watched the city pass,
All now the swallow-gleam of limousines,
And all around her now the boarding house,
Or institutes for drunkards, hideous blocks
Of offices and warehouses.

And all her neighbors lying up in Rose Hill.
Perhaps a few remaining who remembered
All that she was, could only say to those

THE BAY-WINDOW

Who had heard of her as she was in the eighties,
And in the nineties:
"She was a great woman, I can scarce explain.
It was this way: Chicago then was young.
Chicago in ten years is changed all through.
You see it was this way: But then you see
This great two million thing has slipped away
From all our hands."

And then perhaps
A limousine would pass with reckless pridelings
Coming from tea or dancing at the Blackstone,
And find their laughter shortened by her face
At this bay-window
Would say: "Who's that old woman at the window?
She always has a book, or has a fan."

MAN OF OUR STREET

This Man's life had four stages as I hear.
The first stage took him through the days of school
And fastened on his name a prophecy
That he would win success.   The second stage
Took him to thirty years while he was fumbling
The strings to find the key and play in key.
The third stage marked discouragement, departure
To speculations and to reconcilement
That he was born no lawyer.   And the fourth
Was one of quietude and trivial days.
I knew him in this fourth stage as a man
Emerging from a house across the street
On Sunday mornings in silk hat, long coat
And bamboo cane.   When summer came he donned
A flannel suit of gray, a panama
And gloves of tan.   When winter came he wore
A double-breasted coat with lamb's fur collar.
He had no friends, so far as one could see,
No membership in clubs, was never seen
Where men meet, or society is gathered.
Sometimes he stopped to tell a passer-by
The day is fine, it's very fine, you're right,
In voice complaisant.   The neighbors knew

MAN OF OUR STREET

He lived upon a little purse he made
In compromise of some preposterous wrong.
And people wondered how the purse was lasting,
And wondered how much longer he could loaf,
How many seasons more he could appear
So seasonably attired and walk the streets
In such velleity, with such vacuous light
Grown steady in his eyes.

               I love to watch
The chickens in a barn-yard.   Nothing else
Is quite so near the human brood.   You'll see
Invariably a rooster stalk about
In aimless fashion, moving here and there,
Picking at times with dull inappetence
At grains or grit, or standing for a time
In listless revery.   I never saw
A man with such resemblance to this rooster
As this man was.

             At last we had not seen
Our man upon the street for several days.
And some one said he had been very ill.
His wife had fears and wept and said 'twas hard
Just on the eve of great success to die.
He had thought out a plan, she said, to win
Great trade in South America for us.
Our State Department thought it excellent.

And then one day four doctors passed his door
For consultation, and the word went round
Our man rebelled most piteously and said
He could not die until he had worked out
His dream of South America.   He knew
His danger, had the doctors called to check
The inroads of the peril, though the purse
Was growing slim, as we discovered later.

One noon-time as I came along the street
Where twenty children laughed and followed me,
Half playing at their game, half following
My banterings and idle talk, and asking
About the bundle underneath my arm.
"It's nothing but a chicken, go away,"
I said to them.

       And there across the street
Was crape upon the door — our man was dead,
And I was carrying chicken home to boil.

ACHILLES DEATHERIDGE

"Your name is Achilles Deatheridge?
How old are you, my boy?"
"I'm sixteen past and I went to the war
From Athens, Illinois."

"Achilles Deatheridge, you have done
A deed of dreadful note."
"It comes of his wearing a battered hat,
And a rusty, wrinkled coat."

"Why didn't you know how plain he is?
And didn't you ever hear,
He goes through the lines by day or night
Like a sooty cannoneer?"

"You must have been half dead for sleep,
For the dawn was growing bright."
"Well, Captain, I had stood right there
Since six o'clock last night."

"I cocked my gun at the swish of the grass
And how am I at fault
When a dangerous looking man won't stop
When a sentry hollers halt?"

"I cried out halt and he only smiled
And waved his hand like that.
Why, any Johnnie could wear the coat
And any fellow the hat."

"I hollered halt again and he stopped
And lighted a fresh cigar.
I never noticed his shoulder badge,
And I never noticed a star."

"So you arrested him? Well, Achilles,
When you hear the swish of the grass
If it's General Grant inspecting the lines
Hereafter let him pass."

SLIP SHOE LOVEY

You're the cook's understudy
A gentle idiot body.
You are slender like a broom
Weaving up and down the room,
With your dirt hair in a twist
And your left eye in a mist.
Never thinkin', never hopin'
With your wet mouth open.
So bewildered and so busy
As you scrape the dirty kettles,
O Slip Shoe Lizzie
As you rattle with the pans.
There's a clatter of old metals,
O Slip Shoe Lovey,
As you clean the milk cans.
You're a greasy little dovey,
A laughing scullery daughter,
As you slop the dish water,
So abstracted and so dizzy,
O Slip Shoe Lizzie!

So mussy, little hussie,
With the china that you break,

[95]

And the kitchen in a smear
When the bread is yet to bake,
And the market things are here —
O Slip Shoe Lovey!

You are hurrying and scurrying
From the sink to the oven,
So forgetful and so sloven.
You are bustling and hustling
From the pantry to the door,
With your shoe strings on the floor,
And your apron strings a-draggin',
And your spattered skirt a-saggin'.

You're an angel idiot lovey,
One forgives you all this clatter
Washing dishes, beating batter.
But there is another matter
As you dream above the sink:
You're in love pitter-patter,
With the butcher-boy I think.
And he'll get you, he has got you
If he hasn't got you yet.

For he means to make you his,
O Slip Shoe Liz.
And your open mouth is wet
To a little boyish chatter.

SLIP SHOE LOVEY

You're an easy thing to flatter
With your hank of hair a-twist,
And your left eye in a mist —
O Slip Shoe Lovey!

So hurried and so flurried
And just a little worried
You lean about the room,
Like a mop, like a broom.
O Slip Shoe Lovey!
O Slip Shoe Lovey!

THE ARCHANGELS

Flopped on the floor
With such a silken richness of dark hair,
Descending breezily like blown water from her brow,
And from the arched crown of her Raphael head,
Between the years of twenty-five and thirty,
Her face glows and is white,
Like the thin spirit of a candle light.
And over her forehead passes
Swift waves of splendor, which must be her thought,
Looking, it seems, as if a snowy curtain
Were rhythmically blown at dawn in a white room!

In each of her eyes there is a blue-bright spark!
One time I saw two stars
Held in an inch of water when the evening
Was pale from dying day.
And under this thin water lay dead leaves
The drift of late October —
Gray leaves beneath clear water by an edge
Where spring's first flower, the azure pickerel weed,
Bent over contemplated those two stars:
These were the sparks in her unruffled eyes.

THE ARCHANGELS

Flopped on the floor
With little hands clasped round her girlish knees
Such musical thought sings through her cherub lips —
Raptures for Beauty,
Raptures for Truth,
Raptures for Freedom and a world that is free.
While around her flames the fire of a durable hope.
Till at last I sit in wonder
At the miracle of such spirit,
And the miracle of the youths about her,
Listening with bright eyes, in the fellowship of delight,
Who prompt, suggest, applaud, are passionate
For the right word, the soaring thought to beat
At heaven's gate in a last burst of song.
And here am I a part of this psychic circle,
Bound with soft loops of gold in a charméd band
Of a brood of youthful archangels fiery and strong. . . .

Then thrilled with love of a land that can grow such
        souls
I turn and ask them questions:
How old are you, who were your father and mother?
What chance have you had in life?
What books have you read?
And where have you bred these dreams?
But why do you laugh? for there must be soil or blood
Or both, for there must be the souls of free men
And the loins of free men,

To make archangels you know,
And pour them into the city to think and plan
For a greater Republic to come.
And though it matters nothing that villages
In Iowa, Indiana, Illinois
In the great far west, in New England, gave us you,
Or you, or you, or you —
I somehow thrill at the contrast, or thrill with the
    thought
Of such great richness and vastness in the land,
Flowering such souls all fresh and keen,
And eager to make the Republic wholly free —
May she deserve your love!

SONG OF CHANGE

Deep thought that comes through stainless skies;
Pure moods that arch the fancy's birth;
Sweet sorrow, clear in youthful eyes;
Soft laughter, speaking maiden mirth; —
Such gifts were thine, ere time o'ercast
The sunshine of thy tender heart;
And now that joy itself is past
Yet patience still will do its part.

Sad stars from which the sun has drawn
The light of life, no longer bright;
Life of our lives, that with the dawn
Passed, though remembered, from our sight!
From noonday stept the chilling shade
That struck the quivering aspens still;
Thou hopeful one, thou unafraid,
Smiled — but the Shadow had his will.

Souls of our youth which tire and sleep
And wake to find the hour is sped!
Thou scorn which mocks us if we weep!
Thou hope which says "Be comforted!"
Thou vision dulled, whose tutored eye
Sees but in vain the poplar tree
As once upblown against the sky,
When we were fain, when we were free.

MEMORABILIA

Old pioneers, how fare your souls to-day?
They seem to be
Imminent about this pastoral way,
This sunny lea.
The elms and oaks you knew, greenly renew
Their leaves each spring,
But never comes the hour again which drew
Your world from view.

Here in a mood I lay, deep in the grass,
Between the graves;
And saw ye rise, ye shadowy forms, and pass
O'er the wind's waves;
Sunk eyes and bended head, wherefrom is fled
The light of life;
Even as the land, whose early youth is dead,
Whose glory fled.

With eighty years gone over what remains
For tongue to tell?
Hence was it that in silence, with no pains
At last 'twas well,
Under these trees to creep, for ultimate sleep
To soothe regret,

MEMORABILIA

For the world's ways, for war, let mankind reap,
You said, and weep.

Abram Rutledge died, ere the great war
Ruined the land.
His well-loved son was struck on fields afar
By a brother's hand.
Then brought they him, O pioneer, on his bier
To the hill and the tree,
Back home and laid him, son of Trenton, here
Your own grave near.

Of all unuttered griefs, of vaguest woes,
None equals this:
Forgotten hands, and work that no one knows
Whose work it is;
Good gifts bequeathed, but never earned, or spurned
In hate or pride;
And the boon of an age destroyed, ere a cycle turned
O'er you inurned.

Abram Rutledge lies in a sunken grave,
Dust and no more,
Let Freedom fail, it is naught to him, who was brave,
Who stood to the fore.
The oaks and elms he knew, greenly renew
Their leaves each spring,
But gone his dream with that last hour which drew
His world from view.

TO A SPIROCHAETA

If through the microscope
   We peer and stare
You look like marceled shreds of rope,
   Or maiden hair,
With eyeless hunger swift to grope
   Out of your lair.

To feed and to fulfill your fate
   You dive and swim
Forward and backward flagellate
   Amid the dim
Ichor of women where you mate,
   Delicate, slim.

Why are you screw-shaped, in a spiral?
   And why your form
Like a crooked hand upon a dial?
   You are the norm
For all hell sealed up in a vial
   To break in storm.

Your whips are sharper far than sickles,
   Or cricket bristle;

[104]

TO A SPIROCHAETA

With finer points than rose-leaf prickles,
  Or drifting thistle;
You feed yourself till the blood trickles
  Through flesh and gristle.

When a man knows he is your diet
  A solemn thrill
Shows in great eyes and spirit quiet
  For fears that kill;
He is a maelstrom running riot,
  At the center still.

Well, Robert Burns: You saw a louse
  On a lady crawling.
But one can keep to his own house
  Without forestalling
This demon on his death carouse
  Breeding and sprawling.

But, Robert Burns, this does not tent
  Our pride or tease us;
It is not heaven's message sent
  That virtue frees us.
It shows us hard or penitent
  As Nature sees us!

CATO BRADEN

I went to Winston Prairie to attend
The funeral of Cato Braden. He
Had died at fifty-one and I had known him
Since he was twenty-four, but for fifteen
Years or more I had not seen him, nor
Exchanged with him more than a telegraphic
Note about some trivial thing. Indeed
I had not been in Winston Prairie during
These fifteen years.

                    But on the train I thought
Of Cato Braden, brought back all the days
Through which I knew him, from the very first
When he returned to Winston Prairie from
De Pauw, or was it Valparaiso? Yet
'Twas called a university I remember.
And when I knew him first he kept at hand
De Senectute, also Anthon's Homer,
And lexicons in Latin and in Greek,
Both unabridged. Sometimes he let me read
The orations he had won the prizes with.
And sometimes he would tell me what it meant
To study at a university.
And what they did and what the boys were like.

CATO BRADEN

This Cato Braden was a happy soul
At twenty-four, of a full noble brow,
A gentle smiling mouth, an honest eye,
A tall and handsome figure, altogether
A man conspicuous for form, a bearing
Of grace and courtliness, engaging ways;
He might be called most lovable, he had
The gift of friendship, was not envious,
Could scarcely be enraged, was not offended
By little things and often not by great.
He had in short a nature fit to work
With great capacity; had he combined
An intellect but half his nature's worth
He might have won the race.   But many thought
He promised much, his father most of all
Because he had these virtues, and in truth
Before his leaves unfolded with the spring
His mind seemed apt, perhaps seemed measured full
Of quality, the prizes he had won
At Valparaiso pointed to the fruit
He would produce at last.

                              So on the train
I thought of Cato Braden.   Then I thought
Of when he came from school with his degree,
And for that summer when he walked the square,
Was whispered of as "Cato Braden, look."
The first thing Winston Prairie knew it saw

His name conjoined with that of Jerry Ott's —
It was Ott and Braden, editors and owners,
The Winston Prairie Eagle.   Jerry Ott
Was sixty-nine and wheezy from the fight
For Jefferson Democracy, free trade.
Besides the capital that Cato Braden
Brought through his father to the enterprise   .
Meant bitter war on enemies of truth.
And Cato Braden's father had some wealth
Made from the making of a vermifuge
And a preposterous compound which he called
Pesodorne; and I have always thought
That Cato Braden's father garrisoned
His factory for making patent nostrums
By buying for his son this interest,
And place of power in journalism; for
The father's strong devotion to the church
Did not protect him 'gainst the casual sneers
Of Winston Prairie's paper called the Lance,
Which used to print such things as this, to instance:
"There's Braden's Vermifuge, well, Doctor Braden,
Try your own vermifuge, let's see it work."

Well, anyway I know that Cato Braden
Intended to pursue a legal course,
And practice the profession in a city.
I know his father bought for him this place
With Jerry Ott as editor of the Eagle.

CATO BRADEN

I know he went to work.   I know he changed
The paper's motto from "Hew to the line,"
To *Principia non homines*.   I know
He used to sing "Over the Garden Wall,"
While writing editorials and smoked
A number of cheroots.   I know he had
A locked drawer where he kept a secret bottle
From which he'd take a drink at noon or night.
I know he was on terms of friendship with
The milliner and dressmaker in a month
After he came from Valparaiso.   Yes,
I know he advocated a gymnasium,
And dancing hall for Winston Prairie, and
He opened up a fight to get a park
Where concerts might be given.   Cato Braden
Had these ideas at least.   About this park
A word remains to say.

                   Fernando Winston,
Who founded Winston Prairie and surveyed
The original town, laid out a square along
The river for a pleasure ground; in time,
Some fifty years or more, it was forgotten.
And when this Cato Braden came to town
And started as a journalist 'twas used
In part by Winston Prairie's creamery;
In part 'twas used for gardening by the pastor
Of Winston Prairie's strongest church.   But Cato

Had searched the records, found them straight, began
To agitate the park.   And it was this,
Together with *Principia non homines*,
Free trade, the dressmaker and milliner,
Perhaps the bottle in the drawer, whose secret
Leaked out at once, that clove the people of
The town into two groups of friends and foes.
He had but just begun his editorship
When I left Winston Prairie; after that
Knew little of it, saw him but at times,
Long separated, saw him not at all
For fifteen years before his death, and now
Because I was his friend was on the train
His funeral to attend.

       I drove to Oakland
With Dr. Green and William Smoot the grocer.
'Twas hot without a breeze, the town was still.
The church bell tolled until we reached the grave,
It was the church whose pastor used the square
For gardening.   And on the way I asked
Why Cato Braden died at fifty-one.
"Why, whisky," answered William Smoot, the grocer,
"And women," for he had bad luck they say.
"How is that, Doc, you know?"

         And Dr. Green
After a silence said: "It isn't true.

CATO BRADEN

"He was as sound, so far as that's concerned
"As any of us."

Then I asked again
Why Cato Braden died at fifty-one.
And Dr. Green said laughing, "Well, you know
"They die at thirty-one and forty-one,
"And sixty-one of what killed Cato Braden,
"That's Bright's Disease."

"And whisky brings that on —"
I ventured to assert.

"Sometimes" replied
The man of medicine, "But other things
"Produce it.   There's a man's diathesis;
"There's worry, over-work, sometimes disease
"Suffered in childhood, leaving an effect
"Like soil, all fertilized for such seed as this.
"He should have drunk no whisky, yet he drank
"Not half so much as Winston Prairie thought.
"But you can see if whisky caused this thing
"All whisky drinkers would be sure to have it,
"Or die of it if not killed by a train."

We left the carriage, having reached the place
Where Cato Braden's grave was dug, and stood
Together in a company of fifty
And heard the pastor pray for heaven's lessons

[111]

THE GREAT VALLEY

From Cato Braden's life.   And after that
We separated, made the horses trot
To reach our different destinations.   I
Looked up Will Boyden for a little talk
Before my train left for the city.

                                        Will
Was in his office with his sleeves rolled up,
Cob-pipe in mouth, typing a legal paper,
A narratio in slander, so he said.
He smiled from ear to ear and dropped his work.
"You're here for Cato's funeral," he said,
And added, "It's a shame he had to die,
Damned if it isn't."

                        Then I asked again
Why Cato Braden died at fifty-one,
And Will said: "Winston Prairie, Illinois,
Killed Cato Braden."

                                Tell me what you mean?"
Then Will refreshed his pipe and talked to me:
"I'm fifty-two and good for twenty years
I have no stronger frame than Cato Braden,
But then I got a formula for life
As time went on, and it was one that suited
My nature, and I thrived as you can see.
I have the power to draw the nutriment
Out of this soil, and I get strength thereby

Wherewith to overcome the things that kill.
I work, but then I play, I hunt and fish,
I read and sometimes take a little trip.
I don't drink whisky, not because I fear it,
But I hate putting in myself such fire —
Beer and light wines are pleasant, more like food
Than stimulants.   Well, Cato Braden started
When 'Over the Garden Wall' was all the rage,
'All Coons Look Alike to Me' was my
Key-note for starting.   You know what I mean:
Between my day and his there's just the difference
That lies between waltz time and syncopation;
Between the magic lantern and the movie,
The rattan phaeton and Ford machine.
These new things came along before he died,
But he had made his life for the old things,
Could not adjust himself, De Senectute
And Valparaiso had not taught him how
To reach out in the world from Winston Prairie
And get the new things for his life.   But if
They taught him how he lost the secret here.
For after all a place like Winston Prairie
Will kill your spirit just as surely as
The Island where they cooped up great Napoleon.
In the first place what is a man to do
With life in any place?   That is the problem.
And what could Cato Braden do with life
In Winston Prairie?   First he was as fitted

THE GREAT VALLEY

To be a journalist as I, and if
Endowed to be a journalist, just think
Of editing The Eagle.   But you see
His father was at war then with the Lance
Over that vermifuge and pesodorne.
And under guise of starting him in life
Bought Cato in the paper for the selfish
Purpose of defending vermifuge.
And Cato did it too, and put away
From year to year his dream of studying
The law and practicing in a city.
During which time the poisons of this town
Crept in his blood and stupefied and killed him.
He married Mary Comfort, as you know.
And Mary is — well, what I call a brood-mare,
Although they had no children.   What I mean
She is a well-fleshed woman, sound of nerve,
A help-eat, but she made a loyal wife
Who had two eyes to see what Cato saw,
And never an eye to help him see the things
That lay around him, which he stumbled over.
And marriage to my mind means this to man:
He drains his body out to be a father,
And drains his spirit out to be a husband,
Unless the woman helps him see or feel
More than he sees or feels for self.   Well then
The years went on.   And every day at eight
He could be seen toward his office bent.

CATO BRADEN

At half past ten just as the morning train
Was whistling for the crossing he would go
To get the mail.   Returning he would walk
Along Main Street, slapping the folded News
Against his leg.   He scanned it in his office.
At twelve o'clock he went to dinner, then
As whisky made him eat, he over-ate
And took a nap till two o'clock.   At three
One might discover him at solitaire —
He had clipped from the morning paper quite enough
To keep the boys in copy.   Then at four
He might be sitting at the livery stable,
Or sometimes might be found in that back room
Of Little's restaurant, where a keg of beer
Shipped in was being tapped.   At night perhaps
He might be seen down there on Locust street,
Waiting to enter where the milliner lived.
So passed his life away from twenty-four
To fifty-one.   It's simple enough to ask
Why not write for the Eagle, make it better,
Give ideas to the people, help the town,
Refresh the mind, read, study history,
De Senectute?   Fancy Teddy Roosevelt,
Who's labored for this land with restless gifts,
Tied down in Winston Prairie — well, you can't,
He'd break the ties, and that's the point, you see.
For Cato couldn't break them, had to stay,
Incapable to extract the good that's here,

Susceptible to all the bad that's here;
He was a nose half active
Who enters in a room where gas escapes,
Sits in the room unconscious of the gas
Till he grows sluggish, lies him down to rest
And dies unknowing.   So I say it's true
That Winston Prairie ruined Cato Braden
And killed him in the end.

               You must go see,
Before you leave, our park called Willard Park,
Named after Emma Willard, that devout
Old woman, dead these fifteen years or so.
She left enough to build a granite coping,
Set out some trees, and buy park seats, a stone
Whereon to carve the words, 'The gracious gift
Of Emma Willard.'   Well, this Cato Braden
First talked this park, was first to tell the truth
About this plot of ground.   And more than that
When Cato Braden came here he had dreams:
He wrote at first that boxing, wrestling, racing
Would help this town; that games were needed here;
That Americans seemed ignorant of the art
Of being gay, feeling light-hearted, wise
To play; that they were wise to work and pray,
Fear happiness.   And Cato Braden said
The little town was cursed by just these things,
And many human souls destroyed by them.

CATO BRADEN

These were not thoughts of his, he found them somewhere,
But knew them when he found them, that's his credit.
What though he was a drunk man whom you ask
What road to take, who points and gurgles guttural
Sounds inarticulate? Or better still
What though he was a sick man who in vain
Attempts to make his household orders clear?
For it was true that Cato Braden spoke
About these things at first, then gave them up.
For no one seemed responsive to his plans.
And some there were who sneered, and others said
He'd better help the church, and leave alone
The questions which make bitterness and strife,
Which was their way of speaking of the square
Which Cato tried to make into a park.
They say a lung will turn to stone or steel
When men work in the filings and the dust.
At last the dust of Winston Prairie turned
His soul to dust.

            You see old Jerry Ott
Had left a son his interest in the Eagle,
And Cato Braden died right at his table
While playing solitaire. This son came in
And found him dead, a card clutched in his hand.
The card was, strange enough, the deuce of clubs!
This son was glad that Cato Braden died
For now he runs the Eagle by himself.

This Cato Braden had three strains of thought.
I never met him lately but he talked
Some one of them, at times all three of them.
One was the American town must be improved,
So better to conserve the souls and bodies
Of boys and girls.   And even when the movie,
And other things of this day came along
He still maintained they did not meet the case.
He never said what thing was requisite.
But in a general way I think he meant
A stronger, and more truthful and more natural
Outlook and attitude would save a town
From dust, and mold and death.   For once he said:
"This winter I shall read Grote's History."
He never read it.   But I think he meant
He would find out the secret of the Greeks.
And then he'd say the young, the middle aged
The old made separate spheres of feeling, thought;
And that a town should not be ruled by one,
Should not be governed as all folks were old,
Or young, or middle aged, but each should have
The town for his according to his age,
And thought and vital power, within his sphere
And period of life; these separate spheres
Should move untroubled by the others, move
Free, independent of the other spheres.

I talked with Cato Braden for the last

CATO BRADEN

A week ago last night.   He said to me:
I wake these mornings lately with the thought
Another chance will come to me, that death
Will bring another chance.   And then he said:
This is the way of it.   When you are young
You say in five years I shall take a trip,
See New York City, go abroad perhaps.
When five years pass you do not take the trip.
Then you say in a year I'll take the trip.
And so it goes, while you say in a year,
Next year, next year, until at last you say
No, never now!   Well, now you'd think a man
Would weep when he stands up against the wall,
And knows he cannot climb the wall.   But no,
Something still whispers you will do it yet.
And then you know it must be after death,
In life again, the chance will come to you.
For you know well it is not in this life.
Then Cato Braden said: Not in this life
Shall I read Grote, I could not understand it
After these years in Winston Prairie — still
I have a feeling I shall know about it
Somewhere, somehow.

                  You'd better catch your train.
It's good to see you.   Up there in the city
Think sometimes of the American village and
What may be done for conservation of
The souls of men and women in the village."

WINSTON PRAIRIE

"What made you buy those lots in Winston Prairie?
If you had come to me I could have told you
About the circuit judge, the state's attorney,
The county judge, the county clerk, the treasurer,
The assessors and collectors who belong
To what we call a court-house ring. You know
They run the county, re-elect themselves,
Play with the local bosses, stand in league
With sellers of cement, and brick and lumber,
And with the papers given the public printing,
And with the sharks who buy in property
For taxes sold, and with the intriguing thieves
Who make improvements, levy the assessments
For side-walk, sewers."

                So my friend to me.
"Good land," I answered, "I inherited them,
I did not buy these lots. But apropos
Of what you say, I've wondered what's the matter.
I write and write for statements of my taxes,
And cannot get them. Then I take the train,
And travel through the heat to Winston Prairie.
And I stand before a window asking for them.

WINSTON PRAIRIE

Your property was sold, I am informed.
So I redeem, and go out to the grave-yard
To look at Cato Braden's grave, and then
Catch the next train for home.   A week or so
Elapses and I get a letter — hum!
Winston Prairie — office of the controller;
Your property was sold for special numbered
Two thousand and eighty-six, when you reply
Please mention sale 1019. — Damn these thieves!
So I pay that.   I see! your court-house ring, —
The men who're sworn to enforce the law are those
Who break it, and who use it to despoil you —
Well, let me tell you.

                              In this very June
I went to Winston Prairie on this errand,
And after I had written several times
To get a statement.   I arrived at noon —
And yet the court-house offices were closed,
The treasurer's, the clerk's, controller's, all.
I met a janitor who said: All closed
Till half past one.   That meant I'd miss my train
Back to Chicago, and would have to stay
In Winston Prairie until six o'clock.
I sat down in the hall-way with a curse.
But in a minute there were hideous yells,
Shrieks, curses, as it were of women beaten,
Tortured, or strangled.   So I went to see,

And found a door behind which I could hear
Intolerable tears, the scratching of weak hands
Against the door and wall.   What is the matter?
I hallooed through the door.   O, go to hell
A woman said, you know what is the matter.
I don't, I said, I'll help you if I can.
Then followed sobs and wails, and incoherent
Blubbering of words.   At last I saw a finger
Stuck through the broken plaster by the door,
And leaning down I said: look through at me.
And then I stooped and looking through the crack
Saw a gray eye, which looked as it might be
Of Slavic birth.   But who can read an eye
Shown singly through a crack?   So while I talked
To get the story of these girls in prison,
(For where they were was called the calaboose,
Built in the court-house) some one back of me
Said: They'll be quiet in due time, the cooler
Cools people off.   I turned and saw a man
Who seemed to be a judge, and was a judge,
As I discovered later.   Well, I said,
I cannot bear to see a human being
In such distress and terror — what's their ages?
One's sixteen and one's seventeen, said the judge,
But they are bad ones, so I made the fine
Enough to hold them thirty days.   I asked
What did they do?   They were soliciting,
The judge replied, and here in Winston Prairie

WINSTON PRAIRIE

The law is law and we enforce the law.
We do not do as you do in Chicago.
I felt my heart shut tight its valves and stop,
And was about to say: You are a fool.
You are what some would have America,
You are an Illinoisan, damn your soul.
You are a figure in the court-house ring,
Whereof the tax shark is a figure too.
But then I thought these girls might prove to be
Worth while some time.   But even if they live
Street walkers all their lives, they stone no prophets,
Devour no widows' houses, do less harm
Than court-house rings and judges in the rings.
So this is what I said: May I enquire
What are your Honor's hours for holding court?
And he replied: Court has adjourned till two.
I hold till six o'clock, we do not loaf
As judges in Chicago do, good-day!

Well, then at half past one I paid my taxes,
With interest, penalties and all the costs.
At two o'clock I stood before the bar
And to the judge addressed these words: Your Honor,
I represent Miss Christine Leichentritt,
Miss Garda Gerstenburg, who are in jail
Under your Honor's sentence.   I have seen
The state's attorney, who is satisfied
To let them go, if all the costs are paid.

THE GREAT VALLEY

I went to see him on a matter of taxes,
And this came up.   The state's attorney rose
And said: Your Honor, they are very young,
And though they have been caught before at this,
And warned that Winston Prairie is no place
For them to ply their trade, I am inclined
To think they will not break our laws again.

I thought I saw his honor's eye light up
As if it caught a wireless, so he said:
"The court is satisfied."   I paid the costs
And took Christine and Garda to Chicago.
But at the station, as I said good bye,
Christine flared up: You don't suppose that I
Will let you pay those costs, I am not cheap.
I may be bad, but I am square, she said.
And I have money in my room, come on
To Twelfth and Wabash and I'll pay you back
For me and Garda.

                    No, I said, go on.
Try to be good, but if you can't be good,
Be wise, and do not go to Winston Prairie.
I turned and disappeared among the crowds.

WILL BOYDEN LECTURES

The Sunday after Cato Braden died
Will Boyden lectured in the Masons' Hall
Upon the theme, "Was Jesus Really Great?"
At first he pointed out that Jesus knew
No history except that of the Jews.
And if he'd heard of Athens never spoke
A word about it, never read a line
Of Homer, Sophocles, or Aristotle,
Or Plato, or of Virgil, never a word
Concerning Egypt's wisdom, or of India's.
And then he dropped this point with the remark
That one could know one's people's history
And that alone, and still be great, perhaps.
But still he thought it was unfortunate
That Jesus gave the Hebrews such a lift
So that to-day they rule the Occident
Where Athens should have ruled, if only Time
Had given her the right dramatic touch
To catch the populace.

                        He then declared
That Jesus was a poet, but he said:
"What are his figures?   Never a word of stars,
And never a word of oceans, nor of mountains

Save Olivet or Zion, so you see
His limitations as to imagery.
Then have you noted how his sombre soul
Picked blasted fig-trees, tares, the leprous poor,
And sepulchres and sewers, dirty cups,
Wherewith to make interpretations, yes
He spoke of lilies, too.   Well, so have I.
And yet you people call me pessimist
Because I've tried to rescue Winston Prairie,
And have not shrunk from charging Winston Prairie
With Cato Braden's death.   The difference
Between the Man of Galilee and me
Is this: He wanted to fulfill the law
Of Moses and Isaiah, make Jerusalem,
Which was a Winston Prairie in a way,
A Hebrew citadel to rule the world.
And I, if I could have my way, would make
Of Winston Prairie Athens."

                    Then he said
"I have four thoughts to-day to touch upon.
The first one is concerning hogs — you start:
Well, look at Matthew chapter eight and find
How certain hogs had cast in them the devils
Of fierceness, blindness, lustfulness and ran
Down in the sea to kill themselves for being
Made perfecter as hogs.   Go get some hogs
And let me try my hand at exorcising

WILL BOYDEN LECTURES

The Winston Prairie devils which destroyed
Poor Cato Braden.

                    "My next thought is found
In Matthew chapter nine; and it is this;
When Jesus saw the multitude all fainting,
And scattered abroad as sheep without a shepherd,
His soul was stirred — that is a way with genius,
Whether it be your Altgeld, Pericles,
Or yet your artist soul like Heinrich Heine.
But think of this: If you would lead and save
The multitude, assuming that can be,
Shall you accomplish it by rules and laws
Applied externally, which is the way
Ecclesiastic powers pursue and find
Divine authority in Jesus for it?
Or shall you teach the way of opening up
The soul of man to sun-light, letting in
The Power which is around us, in the which
We live and move, and so give chance for growth
To what is in us?   For your shepherd drives.
No, Jesus hit it better when he spoke
Of leaven than of shepherds.

                    "So if one
Find leaven and would give it, let there be
A few to watch the final hour with him,
When he would be delivered from the cup,
But knows it cannot be, that to refuse
The cup is to deny the inexorable law.

THE GREAT VALLEY

"So now I come to what is chiefest here:
Destroy this temple and I will re-build it
In three days.   Now you know what preachers say:
This means the resurrection — not at all!
These were the greatest words that Jesus said.
And here his genius seized its fullest power,
Here was it that he hid Jerusalem
Under his hands as if it were a toy,
And tossed the world up as it were a ball.
Why, what are temples, cities, cultures, ages
Of beauty, glory, but the work of genius?
What earth and stone and flesh but plastic stuff
Responsive to the touch of prophet hands?
What Winston Prairie, what America
And all this turbulence of bobbing heads
In fields and markets, temples, halls across
This continent of sovereign states but puppets
Which may be changed in flesh, in deepest spirit,
Made more erect, heroic, God-like, wise
By genius' hands, not revolutionists',
Nor shepherds'.   So destroy America,
But not by picks and axes, let it be
As in the movies where a lovelier face
Steals in and blots with brighter light a face,
Which must fade out to let the lovelier face
Complete the story.

                    Now in a moment's silence
Let's pray for Cato Braden."

THE DESPLAINES FOREST

The sun has sunk below the level plain,
And yet above the forest's leafy gloom
The glory of the evening lightens still.
Smooth as a mirror is the river's face
With Heaven's light, and all its radiant clouds
And shadows which against the river's shore
Already are as night.   From some retreat
Obscure and lonely, evening's saddest bird
Whistles, and beyond the water comes
The musical reply, and silence reigns —
Save for the noisy chorus of the frogs,
And undistinguished sounds of faint portent
That night has come.   There is a rustic bridge
Which spans the stream, from which we look below
At Heaven above, till revery reclaims
The mind from hurried thought and merges it
Into the universal mind which broods
O'er such a scene.   Strange quietude o'erspreads
The restless flame of being, and the soul
Beholds its source and destiny and feels
Not sorrowful to sink into the breast
Of that large life whereof it is a part.
What are we?   But the question is not solved

THE GREAT VALLEY

Here in the presence of intensest thought,
Where nature stills the clamor of the world,
And leaves us in communion with ourselves.
Hence to the strivings of the clear-eyed day
What take we that shall mitigate the pangs
That each soul is alone, and that all friends
Gentle and wise and good can never soothe
The ache of that sub-consciousness which is
Something unfathomed and unmedicined?
Yet this it is which keeps us in the path
Of some ambition cherished or pursued;
The still, small voice that is not quieted
By disregard, but ever speaks to us
Its mandates while we wake or sleep, and asks
A closer harmony with that great scheme
Which is the music of the universe.

So as the cherubim of Heaven defend
The realms of the unknown with flaming swords,
Thence are we driven to the world which is
Ours to be known through Art, who beckons us
To excellence, and in her rarer moods
Casts shadowy glances of serener lands,
Where all the serious gods, removed from stress
And interruption, build, as we conceive,
In fellowship that knows not that reserve
Which clouds the hearts of those who wish to live
As they, in that large realm of perfect mind.

THE GARDEN

I do not like my garden, but I love
The trees I planted and the flowers thereof.
How does one choose his garden?   O with eyes
O'er which a passion or illusion lies.
Perhaps it wakens memories of a lawn
You knew before somewhere.   Or you are drawn
By an old urn, a little gate, a roof
Which soars into a blue sky, clear, aloof.
One buys a garden gladly.   Even the worst
Seems tolerable or beautiful at first.
Their very faults give loving labor scope:
One can correct, adorn; 'tis sweet to hope
For beauty to emerge out of your toil,
To build the walks and fertilize the soil.
Before I knew my garden or awoke
To its banality I set an oak
At one end for a life-long husbandry,
A white syringa and a lilac tree,
Close to one side to hide a crumbling wall,
Which was my neighbor's, held in several
Title and beyond my right to mend —
One cannot with an ancient time contend.

THE GREAT VALLEY

Some houses shadowed me. I did not dream
The sun would never look o'er them and gleam,
Save at the earliest hour. So all the day
One half my garden under twilight lay.
Another soul had overlooked the shade:
I found the boundaries of a bed he made
For tulips. Well, I had a fresher trust
And spent my heart upon this sterile dust.
What thing will grow where never the sun shines?
Vainly I planted flowering stalks and vines.
What years to learn the soil! Why even weeds
Look green and fresh. But if one concedes
Salvia will flourish not, nor palest phlox
One might have hope left for a row of box.

Why is it that some silent places thrill
With elfin comradeship, and others fill
The heart with sickening loneliness? My breast
Seems hollow for great emptiness, unrest
Casting my eyes about my garden where
I still must live, breathing its lifeless air.
Why should I have a garden anyway?
I have so many friends who pass the day
In streets or squares, or little barren courts,
I fancy there are gardens of all sorts,
Far worse than mine. And who has this delight:
There's my syringa with its blooms of white!
It flourishes in my garden! In this brief

THE GARDEN

Season of blossoms and unfolding leaf
What if I like my garden not but love
The oak tree and the lilac tree thereof,
And hide my face, lest one my rapture guess,
Amid the white syringa's loveliness?

THE TAVERN

(*For my daughter Madeline*)

Nothing disturbed my night of sleep,
I wonder that I ever woke
It was so heavy, was so deep
I scarce had heard the thunder-stroke.
So what was drinking, feasting, talking
By guests who came and guests who went,
Or those who spent the time in walking
The halls and rooms in argument
About the Tavern? Some declared
No better Tavern could be built.
And others called it a deception,
Its purest gold but thinnest gilt,
A cruel cheat considering
No other Tavern gave reception
To folks who might be wayfaring
Anywhere in the whole wide land.

I woke a stranger to it all,
But quickly grew to understand
The ways and customs which prevailed:
Those who won favor, those who failed;
What feasting rooms had echoed laughter;

THE TAVERN

What kisses stolen in what hall;
What corners where the old had cried;
What stairways where the breathless bride
Paused for a moment just to toss
Among the bridesmaids her bouquet;
What rooms where men in work or play
Approved or cursed for gain or loss
The Tavern's roof-tree, roof and rafter.

Then when I woke, as I have said,
Save a few children there was none
Who was not older far than I.
Many were trembling gray of head;
The strong walked forth in rain or sun
And seemed all danger to defy.
All welcomed me and called me fair,
And told me strange events which passed
Around the Tavern while I slept.
Soon there were changes.   Scarce aware
Of their departure many stept
Out of the door and seemed to cast
Their fortunes elsewhere, but as fast
New guests came in to take the places
Of those who left.   And through the day
I lost the old, remembering faces
Freshly arrived.   When it was noon
I knew what things were opportune,
I had become one of the crowd

THE GREAT VALLEY

In all their ways initiate:
Knew what their love was, what their hate,
Myself stole kisses in the hall,
And saw the old who sat and cried
In corners, saw the rosy bride
Pause for a moment just to toss
Among the bridesmaids her bouquet,
Where I stood best man to the groom.
Was myself of the noisy room,
Where men in work or men in play
Approve or curse the gain or loss.

Toward afternoon I seemed to feel
More people knew me than I knew.
Then it was good to meet with you.
I saw you as you left the stair.
And who were you ?   I do not dare
To praise your brow, or paint your hair,
Your eyes how gray, or were they blue?
A pain strikes through me if I let
The full strength of my love have sway.
I only know I can forget
All others who had gone away
Remembering our happy day
Together in the house and yard.
It was to you all fair and new.
You listened with such rapt regard
To all the stories of the guests,

THE TAVERN

And what had been their interests.
And was the Tavern just the same
As it had been before you came,
You asked me, and I answered, yes,
No change, my dear, not even the name.

No change, except the people change,
And change they do, I must confess.
In truth a few alone remain
Of those who lived here when I first
Entered the door there, most are strange.
And as I rose much earlier
Than you arose, you may suppose
I shall grow drowsy, yet who knows
Before you do, and leave the stir
The dancing, feasting, just to creep
Back for another night of sleep.
I'd like so well to stay awake
And watch the dancing for your sake.
It may be, though it scarce may be —
No one remained awake for me.

You cannot fail to find the bed
When you are sleepy, but no doubt
It will be black with the light out.
Come dear, that sleep is loveliest
Where side by side two lovers rest,
That sweetens sleep — it may be best!

O SAEPE MECUM

(*For E. J. S.*)

Edward! you knew the city and you knew
Where dancing and where music were,
And every hall and theatre,
And every green purlieu

Of gardens where beneath the vines and trees
One might sip beer and be consoled
By music mixed with talk, behold
The summer's devotees

About the tables, idling June away.
And you knew chicory and cress,
With French or Mayonnaise could dress
A salad, growing gay

As you poured Burgundy or Rhenish wine,
Or had a sirloin brought to see
If it were ripe, the recipe
For broiling it, to dine

Thereon in fitting state, the waiter took
And bowed in admiration, then
You snapped your silver case again
And from the holders shook

O SAEPE MECUM

Such cigarettes as Turkish grandees smoke,
And blew the perfumed incense forth,
Descanting on our life, the worth
Of lawyers, noted folk:

Of judges, politicians, governors,
Until the dinner came at last.
And there amid the rich repast
We poor solicitors

Gloried in life, and ruddy faced would laugh
At any mishap, any fate
That we could fancy might await,
And glorying would quaff

Incredible goblets of the quickening juice,
With blackest coffee topping all,
And afterwards a cordial —
Nothing we could abuse

And nothing hurt us, Edward! It was well
We lived, I think, and memories stored:
For now I am a little bored
With the invariable

And settled round of nights and days wherein
I must have sleep to work, and keep
Abstemious to work and sleep —
While you long since have been

THE GREAT VALLEY

The tangled lion of a woman's hair
Who reads you novels and the news,
And mends you, tends you, even brews
Your broth and gives you care

In these dyspeptic mornings.   As for me
The cafés, gardens haunt me yet.
I go about as one who can't forget
A dead felicity —

The Bismarck, Rector's where I enter not —
The music all is changed — and where
No faces that we knew are there,
And where we are forgot.

MALACHY DEGAN

Malachy, you stand a referee to judge
Under a torrent of blue light
The naked pugilists who fight,
Grim faces with a smudge

Of blood, or on the sliding arms or backs,
There on a platform roped, in palls
Of smoke to the roof of Tattersall's,
And where the iterant cracks

Of matches struck for lights prick through the hum
Of voices over toned by cries
Of "Finish him," "Look at his glassy eyes,"
"That sounded like a drum."

When the timekeeper's gong went clang! clang!
And a hush came over us, as then
Bath robes slipped off, the fighting men
Out of their corners sprang,

And in between the tangled arms and legs,
And clinches which you break, you glide
Red-haired, athletic, watchful eyed,
And like a lager keg's

[141]

Round fulness is your chest, your arms all bare,
Coatless, a figure memorable.
You should not be forgotten — well
And if it be to dare

The censure of a taste American
To celebrate your courage, wit,
I write you down what here is writ:
A referee, a man!

A judge who loved the game and whose decree
Had no taint on it, was more pure
Than much of our judicature,
Of every knavery free.

And what is here to shock or shake such nerves
As children's are, delicate women's?
There goes the short hook of Fitzsimmons,
And Thorne a moment swerves,

Then topples over, and lies quiet while
You count from one slowly to nine.
And Thorne lies there without a sign
Of life, but with a smile

After a time gets up, and reels across
The ring to his own corner, there
Flops wobbly in his corner's chair,
And wonders at his loss.

MALACHY DEGAN

While full ten thousand cheer, and watch you shake
The master hand, the general's.
Such was our sport at Tattersall's
Before the Puritan rake

Combed through the city.   Now the sport is dead,
And you are dust these several years.
And we who drift to stale careers,
And live along and tread

The old deserted ways we loved and knew,
Ask sometimes how it was a cough
Could seize upon you, take you off —
A lad as strong as you?

MY DOG PONTO

If I say to you "Come, Ponto, want some meat?"
You laugh in your dog-way and bark your "Yes."
And if I say "Shall we go walking" or
"Stand up, nice Ponto," then you stand up, or
If I say to you "Lie down" you lie down.
You know what meat is, what it is to walk.
You see the meat perhaps or get an image
Of scampering on the street or chasing dogs
While sniffing in fresh air, exploring bushes.
Upon these levels our minds meet at once,
As if they were the same stuff for such thoughts.
But if I look into your eye and say:
I'll read to you a chapter on harmonics,
Here's mad Spinoza's close wrought demonstration
Of God as substance, here is Isaac Newton's
Great book on gravitation, here's a thesis
Upon the logos, of the word made man.
Or if I say let's talk about my soul —
Since I have talked to yours in terms of meat —
Which sails out like a spider on its thread
Through mathematics, music, — look at you
You merely lie there with half open eye,
And thump your tail quite feebly just because,

MY DOG PONTO

And for no other reason save I'm talking,
And I'm your master and you're fond of me,
And through affection would no doubt be glad
To know what I am saying, as 'twere meat
I might be saying. But I know a way
To make you howl for things not understood:
It makes you howl to hear my new Victrola
With a Beethoven record, why is this?
Perhaps this is to you a maddening token
Of realms that lie above the realms of meat,
And torture you because they have suggestions
Of things beyond you.

                   But in any case,
Dear Ponto, if you were an infidel
You might say "What's harmonics? they're a joke."
"And who's Spinoza, Newton, they are myths."
"And mathematics, music, can you eat them,"
"For what you cannot eat has no existence."
Deny them as you will these spheres of thought
Lie as the steps of mountains over you.
They wait for you to gain them, you can find them
By rising to them, then how real they are!
As real as scampering when I take a walk.
But are they all? How do I know what spheres
Of life lie all around me and above me,
Just waiting not for me, but till I climb
And rest awhile and take their meaning in.

THE GREAT VALLEY

How do I know what hand plays a Victrola
With records greater than Beethoven's song,
Which make me howl as piteously as you?
But here again our minds meet on a level:
I know no more than you do why I howl;
Nor what it is that makes me howl, nor why,
Though not content with meat, I want to know,
And keep as all my own this higher music.

THE GOSPEL OF MARK

How long have you been waiting? Not so long?
I'm glad of that. You found the place at once.
Well, there's the Campus Martius, when you're there
You see above this Collis Hortulorum,
A good place for two men like us to meet:
Here's where luxurious souls have their abodes.
That's Sallust's garden there. They do not care
So much about us as some others do.
There is a tolerance comes from being rich,
An urbane soul is fashioned by a villa.
Our faith is not to these a wicked thing,
A deadly superstition as some deem it.
But Mark, my son, there's Rome below you there —
What temples, arches, under the full moon!
Here let us sit beside this chestnut tree,
And while the soft wind blows out of the sea
Let's finish up our talks. You must know all
Wherewith to write the story ere I die
Beneath the wrath of Nero. See that light,
Faint like a little candle — I passed there.
That's one of our poor men, they make us lamps
Wherewith to light the streets and Nero's gardens.
We shall be lamps they'll wish to snuff in time.

THE GREAT VALLEY

We met to-night at one Silvanus' house.
And I was telling them about the night
When in Gethsemane you followed Him,
Having a cloth around your naked body.
And how you laid hold on him, left the cloth
And fled. But when you write this you can say
"A certain young man," leaving out your name,
You may not wish to have it known 'twas you
Who ran away, as I would like to hide
How I fell into sleep and failed to watch,
And afterwards declared I knew Him not:
But as for me omit no thing. The world
Will gain for seeing me rise out of weakness
To strength, and out of fear to boldness. Time
Has wrought his wonders in me, I am rock,
Let hell beat on me, I shall stand from now!

Then don't forget the first man that he healed.
There's deep significance in this, my son,
That first of all he'd take an unclean spirit
And cast it out. Then second was my mother
Cured of her fever, just as you might say:
Be rid of madness, things that tear and plague,
Then cool you of the fever of vain life.
But don't forget to write how he would say
"Tell no man of this," say that and no more.
Though I may think he said it lest the crowds
That followed him would take his strength for healing,

And leave no strength for words, let be and write
"Tell no man of this" simply.   For you see
These madmen quieted, these lepers cleaned
Had soon to die, all now are dead, perhaps.
And with them ends their good.   But what he said
Remains for generations yet to come, with power
To heal and heal.   My son, preserve your notes,
Of what I've told you, even above your life.
Make many copies lest one script be lost.
I shall not to another tell it all
As I have told it you.

              But as for me
What merit have I that I saw and said
"Thou art the Christ?"   One sees the thing he
   sees.
That is a matter of the eye — behold
What is the eye?   Is there an Eye Power which
Produces eyes, a primal source of seeing,
An ocean of beholding, as the ocean
Makes rivers, streams and pools, so does this Power
Make eyes?   You take an egg and keep it warm
About a day, then break the shell and look:
You'll find dark spots on either side of what
Will be the head in time, these will be eyes
In season, but just now they cannot see,
Although the Eye Power back of them can see
Both what they are and how to make them eyes

By giving them its quality and strength.
And all the time while these dark spots emerge
From yolk to eyes, this Rome is here no less,
This moon, these stars, this wonder! Take a child
It stares at flowers and tears them, or again
It claws the whiteness of its mother's breast,
Sees nothing but the things beneath its nose.
The world around it lies here to be seen,
And will be seen from boyhood on to age
In different guises, aspects, richnesses
According to the man, for every man
Sees different from his fellow. What's an eye?
I say not what's an eye, but what is here
For eyes to see? What wonders in that sky
Beyond my eye! What living things concealed
Beneath my feet in grass or moss or slime,
As small to crickets as they are to us!
For Nero at the Circus holds a ruby
Before his eye to give his eye more sight
To see the games and tortures. So I say
There was no merit in me when I said
"Thou art the Christ."

               Let's think of eyes this way:
The lawyers said there's nothing in this fellow.
His family beheld no wonder in him.
Have Mary Magdalene and I invented
These words, this story? — who are we to do so,—

THE GOSPEL OF MARK

A fallen woman and a fisherman!
Or did this happen? Did we see these things?
Did Mary see him risen and did I?
Were other eyes still dark spots on the yolk,
And were our eyes full grown and did we see?
Is this a madman's world where I can talk,
And have you write for centuries to read
And play the fool with them? Or do all things
Of spirit, as of stars, of spring and growth
Proceed in order, under law to ends?
No, Mark, my son, this is the truth, so write,
Preserve this story taken from my lips.
My work is almost done. Rome is the end
Of all my labors, I have faith The Eye
Will give me other eyes for other worlds!

Why should I not believe this? Not all seasons
Are for unfolding. In the winter time
You cannot see the miracle of birth,
Of germinating seeds, of blossoming.
Why not then that one time for seeing Death
Go up like mist before the rising sun?
And in this single instance of our Lord
Arising from the grave, see all men rise,
And all men's souls discovered in his soul,
Their quality and essence, strength made clear?
And why not I the seer of these things?
Why should there be another and not I?

And I declare to you that untold millions
In centuries untold will live and die
By these words which you write, as I have told them.
And nation after nation will be moulded,
As heated wax is moulded, by these words.
And spirits in their inmost power will feel
Change and regeneration through them — well, what
    then?
Do you say God is living, that this world,
These constellations, move by law, that all
This miracle of life and light is held
In harmony, and that the soul of man
Moves not in order, but that it's allowed
To prove an anarch to itself, sole thing
That turns upon itself, sole thing that's shown
The path that leads no whither? is allowed
To feed on falsehood? that it's allowed
To wander lawless to its ruin, fooled
By what it craves, by what it feels, by eyes
That swear the truth of what they see? by words
Which you will write from words I have affirmed?
And do you say that Life shall prove the foe
Of life, and Law of law? Or do you say
The child's eyes see reality which see
The poppy blossoms or the mother's breast,
And this Rome and these stars do not exist
Because the child's eyes cannot compass them,
And get their image? Shall we trust our vision

THE GOSPEL OF MARK

Mounting to higher things, or only trust
Those things which all have seen except the souls
Who have not soared, or risen to the gift
Of seeing what seemed walking trees grow clear
As men or angels? No, it cannot be.
Man's soul, the chiefest flower of all we know,
Is not the toy of Malice or of Sport.
It is not set apart to be betrayed,
Or gulled to its undoing, left to dash
Its hopeless head against this rock's exception,
No water for its thirst, no Life to feed it,
No law to guide it, though this universe
Is under Law, no God to mark its steps,
Except the God of worlds and suns and stars,
Who loves it not, loves worlds and suns and stars,
And them alone, and leaves the soul to pass
Unfathered — lets me have a madman's dream
And gives it such reality that I
Take fire and light the world, convincing eyes
Left foolish to believe. It cannot be. . . .

Go write what I have told you, come what will
I'm going to the catacombs to pray.

MARSYAS

Pallas Athena in an hour of ease
From guarding states and succoring the wise,
Pressed wistfully her lips against a flute
Made by a Phrygian youth from resonant wood
Cut near Sangarius.   Upon a bank
Made sweet by daisies and anemone
She sat with godly wisdom exercised
Blowing her breath against the stubborn tube
That it might answer and vibrate in song.
But while she played, down-looking, she beheld
A serpent's eyes, which by the water's edge
Lay coiled among the reeds, as if aware
Of the divinity that filled the place.
Then Athena saw her image in the cove,
Where like a silver mirror, motionless
Sangarius lay, and seeing her own face
Thus suddenly, was stricken with surprise
Of her fair forehead wrinkled, and her lips
Pursed and distorted as she strove to curb
The resisting instrument.   So with a smile,
A little laugh, which brought her beauty back,
And gilded like a gradual burst of sun
The water where the charmed serpent lay

MARSYAS

Lifting his head up to the living warmth,
She threw the flute down, and Olympus way
Vanished, from sight.

                          Marsyas all the while
Beneath an oak's shade by the water's edge
Had drowsed voluptuously, and heard the notes,
Dreaming some shepherd youth who watched his sheep
Upon a near-by hill which to the swale
Sloped in luxuriance, upon a reed
His idle fancies loosened from the stops.
But when Athena passed him, since he heard
A roar of wings, as when a flock of quail
Up-fly the hunter's step, he woke to find
The forest silent and the music gone.
Then straying toward the rushes, he espied
The flute upon the golden sands, and took it
And tried his lips upon it, where the lips
Of Pallas Athena left it fragrant, moist,
And with a soul, which to the artless breath
Of the rude Satyr gave melodious speech.
So thinking that the music was his own
And that the flute was but a worthless wood
Save that it made his genius manifest,
And swollen with conceit Marsyas sent
A word of challenge to the Delphic god,
Apollo of the cithara, for trial
Of skill in music, saying who should prove

THE GREAT VALLEY

The victor might do with the other what
Pleased him to do, and let the Muses judge.

But when Athena heard Apollo laugh,
Where the nine Muses gossiped of the dare
Which Marsyas uttered, for the lower meadows
Of flowered Olympus whispered of the thing
In jest and quip, and knowing that her soul
Still echoed in the flute, but would anon
Fade from it as the perfume from a girdle
Tinct by the touch of Aphrodite's hand,
Spoke to Apollo: "Grant a little time
Wherein the Satyr may improve his skill."
To which the Muses nodded 'mid their smiles.
But yet Apollo gave assent, though teased
By reason of their chatter and the thought
Hid in Athena's word that any respite
Granted the Satyr could prosper his success.

Meanwhile Marsyas waited for the day
Appointed of Apollo.   Near Sangarius
And through the woodlands tireless with the flute:
Sometimes in imitative harmony
Mocking the sound of fluttering leaves, and now
The musical winds that blow in early spring
Around a peak of dancing asphodel
Where the sea warms them, and at other times
The little waves that patter on the sands

MARSYAS

Of old Sangarius rich in numerous flags.
And once he strove with music's alchemy
To turn to sound the sunlight of the morn
Which fills the senses as illuminate dew
Quickens the ovule of the tiger-flower.
Again he sang the sorrow of his youth
When a wild nymph after one day of bliss
Fled him while sleeping.   And again he beat
The rhythm lying at the root of life
Which marks the whirling planets.   And Apollo
Hearing betimes a note of purest tone
Fall like a star, betrayed his wonderment —
Whereat the muses vexed him with their smiles
And whisperings to each other.   But Apollo
Could sense the Satyr's waning skill, which dulled
With its employment, as Athena's soul
Died from the flute, although the Satyr knew not
Each day of waiting doomed him:

                                    Then at last
The day dawned for the trial of their skill,
And Marsyas came bearing the hollow flute —
For all had left it of Athena's soul.
Then on Sangarius' wooded banks the muses
To judge assembled, fair, majestical.
With arms entwined some close together stood,
Some half-reclined upon the flowery grass,
But all bore in their eyes the light of mirth

Suppressed, half-hidden. Then, for that Euterpe
Was mistress of the flute, since it was deemed
Fair to the Satyr that the contest be
Judged by the flute, gave signal to begin.
Whereat Apollo struck the cithara
To test the strings, and all the wood was hushed,
Awed by the magic of its harmony.
But when Marsyas blew upon the flute
A fear coursed through him as his wonder rose
Whether Apollo had bewitched its soul
To such discordance, or its utterance,
Such as he knew it, when compared with the god's
Was so unmusical.   Yet he dare not fail
The contest, so they waged it to the end,
While the sweet muses now grown pitiful
No longer smiled, but turned their heads away
In sorrow for Marsyas, for his shame
And for the fate to follow.

                              So at last
With one accord the muses rose and looked
With eyes significant upon Apollo,
Who angered by the Satyr's swollen pride
And monstrous failure, had become a will
Of resolute retribution.   But the muses,
Because they feel for those who trying lose,
Even as a mother for her crippled son
Whom the sound-footed distance in the race,

MARSYAS

Hastened away lest they behold the thing
That came to pass.   And flinging far the flute
Marsyas shrieked and sank upon the earth.

Whereat Apollo seized his wretched form
And lifting him up, with strips of laurel bark
Bound the poor Satyr to a rugged oak
And flayed him alive, and took the Satyr's skin
And hung it in a cave, and turned his blood
To water, whence the river Marsyas
That from the cave flows onward to this day.

WORLDS BACK OF WORLDS

This was the world: It was a house
With a cool hallway end to end
Where buckets, pans and dippers hung,
And coats that in the breezes swung;
And eaves in which 'twas good to browse
On books stored in a musty box.
Along the walks were lilac boughs,
And by the windows hollyhocks.
And there were fields down to the hills
Which marked the earth's far boundary;
A church-spire at the roadway's bend,
And barns and cribs and twinkling mills,
And neighbor friends like Mrs. Gray,
And endless days of dream and play.
It was a world so guarded, safe,
So cherished by a God-watched sky
Seeing the summers come and pass,
A world so quiet it appeared
Like to the mimic world ensphered
By witchery of the old field glass
Which from an uncle's drawer I took
Upon the distant hills to look.

WORLDS BACK OF WORLDS

You know not then that worlds not dead
Lie back of you and bide their chance
To seize your world of ignorance:
There was an opening in the ceiling
Above the kitchen where the man
Sat humming to himself at night
Amid the enshadowed candle-light,
And played on his accordion
Happy, unconscious and alone.
There full of mischief would I lie
And watch him through the ceiling's hole,
And laugh for thought of elfish tricks,
Of whispering words or dropping sticks
To fright his well contented soul.
Sometimes I think there is an eye
Which is not God's that spies upon us;
That other worlds may lie about us
Our fathers or our mothers lived,
Where Forces lurk and laugh and wait.

Here then was my world's fair estate —
For so I knew it — could it be
Disturbed or wrecked?   I never thought
That change or loss could come to me,
With God above the church's spire. . . .

But what are all these April dreams?
Less tangible the landscape seems;

THE GREAT VALLEY

The windmills, barns and houses swim
In a sphered ether, wheeling, dim.
Red cattle on green meadows pass
Across a belt of bluest sky
Like objects in the old field glass.
The chickens stalk about the yard
Like phantom things in my regard
And songs and cries and voices sound
Like muffled echoes from the ground.
Stones and dead sticks crawl and move;
And bones that through the winter lay
Something of living power betray.
I sink in all things dizzily,
Made one with nature, all I see,
Until I have no way to prove
My separate identity.
Yet death is what?   Why, death is this:
Something that comes but is far off.
They worry sometimes for my cough.
I know they watch me, know they cry,
But what can wreck my earth or sky?

The doctor comes now every day
And with my father sits and talks,
Or stands about the garden walks.
One day I hear them: "It appears
Sometimes in ten or twenty years
As madness or paralysis.

WORLDS BACK OF WORLDS

Sometimes it passes, leaves a scar
And never troubles one again.
You say you had this in the war?
It's hit your boy as phthisis,
Also I think he's going blind."
I saw my father trembling wind
Some plucked grass round and round his hand.
They noticed me, walked further on
And left me dreaming where I sat.

Some years since that day now are gone.
I have no world now, none but night.
My father's world lay back of mine
And wrecked my world so guarded, safe,
So cherished by a God-watched sky
Which looked on summers rise and pass,
So like an image caught and held
By witchery of the old field glass.

THE PRINCESS' SONG

"Blow, blow, thou wind,
Blow Conrad's hat away,
Its rolling do not stay,
Till I have combed my hair,
And tied it up behind."

Blow, blow, thou wind,
Blow Conrad's love away,
My prince will come to-day.
Let him but find me fair,
And searching find.

The queen my mother grieves
For hopes that went astray.
Blow thou my grief away,
Among the April flags,
Among the dancing leaves.

Fill thou their golden wings,
And make the great clouds fly
Like swans across the sky,
Above the mountain crags
Where the young eaglet clings.

THE PRINCESS' SONG

Blow — yet the mad wind dies
Among the flags and ferns.
And Conrad still returns,
Ere I have bound my hair,
Or dried my eyes.

Blow, blow, thou wind —
Blow Conrad's love away.
But since it will not stay,
Blow thou afar my care
And make me kind.

As even, lad, thou art.
Blow, blow, thou wind, but since
Vainly I wait the prince
Come, Conrad, loose my hair, —
Thou loyal heart!

THE FURIES

I

But you must act.   And therein lies the way
Of freedom from the Furies.   You must burn
The substance of your being, if you stay
The impetus of life you will not learn
The simples of salvation.   Go pluck off
A serpent from Alecto's head and laugh
Exhilarate with its poison.   If you scoff
You will perceive.   You cannot love the staff
You have not scorned.   You cannot weigh the act
You have not lived, the fear you did not prove.
Your soul was made to focus and extract
Through action every hatred, every love.
Pour out yourself if you would know release
From what the Furies do to spoil your peace.

II

Ambition that eludes, love never found
High hopes that tempt, or goodness still pursued
Have their own Furies, for this mortal ground
Breeds serpents from the blood of fortitude
And action as it does from listless fear.

[166]

THE FURIES

You have aspired and fallen, curse the past
Till madness come! Be quiet, hide or sear
The memory of the dream, no less at last
The Sisters shall arrive! How do they come?
Your life grows round a moral governance
And you have served it. You are stricken dumb
To see it crumble spite of vigilance.
Now when you cannot think, rebuild, repair
The Sisters come and wheel your cripple's chair.

III

You were a fennel stalk that laughed and grew
With laughter till the life in you could use
The cells no further, then the cold winds blew,
And you fell whispering of the April dews.
Grown fair or foul the rhythmic force was spent,
The summer gone, your little past achieved,
Repulsions balanced, though you might lament
So much neglected, or too much believed.
You were a dry weed when a Great Hand seized
And bore you as a carrier of fire.
The garden you had grown in had not pleased!
Was this, perhaps, the end of your desire?
You lit a heap of leaves where children came,
The Furies meditating watched the flame!

APOLLO AT PHERÆ

Zeus envied Æsculapius that he healed
The sick and brought the dead to life, and fain
Would slay him. So the Cyclops brought Zeus light-
    ning
With which Zeus smote the healer. Then Apollo
Destroyed the Cyclops, grieving for his son.
And Clotho laughed to see the thread of fate
Slip by Atropos, woven in the cloth
Of destiny. For had she cut the thread
Shot from the spindle, then a little trace
Of scarlet, but no figures of despair
Had marked the storied tapestry. So Apollo
Was doomed for punishment to tend the flocks
Of King Admetus, lord of Pheræ. Next
Apollo met a mortal woman, daughter
Of an old soldier, servitor of the gods
And rich in land.

              He, sitting on a rock
That overlooked a green Thessalian field
Where grazed the flocks, clad in a leopard's skin,
His crook beside him, dreamed of wide Olympus:
"This hour the muses dance, the Council sits
And there is high debate, or Hera storms

APOLLO AT PHERÆ

For Zeus' absence; there is life, and I
Unknown, alone, a shepherd by this field
Of pastoral pathos labor all the day."
And then a step disturbed his revery;
And looking up he saw a slender maid
White as gardenias, jonquil-haired, with eyes
As blue as Peneus when he meets the sea.
And an old weakness crept upon the god.
For ever in his soul there shone the face
Of woman, like the face of Artemis,
His virgin sister, delicate and chaste;
And to o'ercome such whiteness and reserve
Had been Apollo's madness from his birth.
And this Chione, daughter of the soldier,
Servitor of the gods and rich in land
At once became his passion.   So he rose
And to Chione spoke, and she, to him.
And then anon she saw the unkept curls
Sun-bleached, that touched his shoulders, then his
    breast,
Smooth as her own, and then his arms, his hands
His shapely knees, his firm and pointed feet,
And her eyes closed as stars beneath the dawn
And dawn rose in her cheeks.   And the god knew
Her inmost thought.

             So all that day they played,
Amid the wind-blown light of Thessaly.

He wove her traps for crickets from the grass,
And from the willow branches made her flutes;
He caught her butterflies, and sang her runes
Of living things, and how the earth and sea
From Erebus and Love sprang into being;
And how the sun, and the bright pageant of the stars
Dance joyously to music.   And Chione
Was dumb for happiness; and the day went by.
But with the dusk there came a swooning languor,
All was forgotten save the shepherd's face
Held close to hers, and round his moving curls
The circled splendor of the sickle moon —
Nor eyes, nor lips, only a golden blur.
And rousing she beheld the enshadowed field
Flockless and silent, and the shepherd gone.
Then through the night Chione weakly walked
And found at last her home.

                              The light of day
Brought terror to Chione.   Then she sought
And found Apollo where he sat before
And told him that her father, the old soldier,
Was favored of Admetus, and would bring
The royal power against him, if he failed
The troth of wedlock.   And Apollo mused
Upon his exile from Olympus' throne,
And Zeus' wrath against him, that he slew
The Cyclops, and upon his shepherd state

APOLLO AT PHERÆ

Tending Admetus' flocks, and how unknown
And weak he stood between these kingly hands
Of Zeus and of Admetus.   And seeing her fair,
More fair in tears, he gave her his consent.

Next day Chione brought the god a robe
And sandals and a girdle.   Thus arrayed
Chione took him to her father's home
The ancient soldier, servitor of the gods,
And rich in land, and spoke of him as Acteus
A merchant from the city.   Then the father
Gave thanks to Zeus and at the family board
Apollo supped, as one who would become
Chione's husband.   So it came to pass.
They walked together in the bridal train
Behind the perfumed torches.

                              All the while
Zeus smiled to see Apollo's punishment.
And Hera, who with woman's subtlety,
Knew that there shone within Apollo's soul
A face like to the face of Artemis,
His virgin sister, delicate and chaste,
And to o'ercome such whiteness and reserve
Had been Apollo's madness from his birth,
Laughed freely with the muses as she said:
"Thus is the masculine spirit ever caught
By its own lure, let Zeus himself take heed
Lest sometime he be snared."

THE GREAT VALLEY

                    So when Olympus
Grew dull, the gods for fun looked o'er the ramparts
And spied upon Apollo at the board
With all Chione's family; or at night
Beside Chione and the little faces
Which every year increased.   Or on Apollo
About his bitter task of shepherding
To win the bread for faded Chione
And for the children.

                    Thus the nine years passed.
Then Zeus, avenged, sent all the muses down
To bring Apollo back, and to Olympus
Humbled and sorrowful he came again,
With wrinkles and a touch of whitened hair,
And a lack-lustre eye, which all the art
Of Aphrodite after many days
Could scarce remove.

                    Then Chione told her father
That Acteus was not a merchant from the city.
"Too late," she said, "I found he had deceived me
And masked his shepherd calling."

                    To which her father
The ancient soldier, servitor of the gods
And rich in land: "Yea, daughter, he deceived you.
Now he has run away, abandoned you,
May the gods note it and avenge the wrong."

STEAM SHOVEL CUT

Steam Shovel Cut lies through a wood,
And the trestle's at the end.
And north are the lonely Fillmore Hills,
And south the river's bend.

It's Christmas day and the blue on the hill
Is flapped by a flying crow.
And the steel of the railroad track is cold,
And the Cut is piled with snow.

What is that there by the trestle's end
Where the Cut slopes down to the slough?
That's Cora Williams lying there
In her cloak of faded blue.

Her skirt is red as a northern spy,
And her mittens blackberry black.
And under her cotton underskirt
There's a green place on her back.

Her little gray hat is over her brow,
And covers a purple bruise.
She had white stockings for her feet
And the holes were in her shoes.

THE GREAT VALLEY

Where did you meet Croak Carless, girl?
And where did you start to booze?
They saw you once at Rigdon's place,
And last at Sandy Hughes'.

On the night that Jesus Christ was born
You were drinking gin and beer.
They saw you sitting on Carless' knees
As the midnight hour drew near.

They saw you two start into the night,
And the night was cold and black.
And then they found you there by the bridge
With the green bruise on your back.

Down through the dark to the Shovel Cut
The two of you walked and sang.
You were holding hands on the trestle bridge
When the bell began to clang.

'Twas back of the curve that the head-light shone
So what was the use of eyes?
The mad iron thing leaped on you there
As you ran on the trestle ties.

It rushed on you like a furious bull
That charges a scarlet flag.
The engineer looked long at the gauge
As the fireman scraped the slag.

[174]

STEAM SHOVEL CUT

Croak Carless jumped and fell on a stone
And the world to him was a blank.
But the iron thing struck at your back
And doubled you down on the bank.

Croak Carless woke from a sleep like death
And found you covered with blood.
He slinks to the river to wash his hands,
He runs to hide in the wood.

He steals through thickets, hides in a barn,
He cowers where the corn's in shock.
But the posse catches Croak by noon,
And the jailer turns the lock.

Croak Carless' wife weeps at the bars,
Croak weeps in a grated cell.
They've mortgaged the farm for a lawyer's fee
To save Croak's soul from hell.

For the Coroner has a bat-like thing
In a bottle safe in his room.
It looks like a baby devil fish —
It's Cora Williams' womb.

A woman's womb is a thing of doom
And winged with a fan-like mesh.
And who was the father, they're asking Croak,
Of this bit of jelly flesh?

And the doctors took an oath in the court
That a sharp club did the deed.
And the judge was a foe of the lawyer man
Croak Carless paid to plead.

And Croak had talked too much in jail,
And he trembled and testified
To a woeful tangle of time and place,
And the jury thought he lied.

Croak Carless' wife sobbed out in court
As they twisted him out and in.
For they made him swear he drank with the girl,
And swear to his carnal sin.

They stood him up on the gallow's trap
And his voice was clear and low:
If I killed Cora Williams, men,
My soul to hell should go.

They sprang the trap, Croak Carless shot
Like a wheat bag toward the floor.
And the doctors let his body hang
Till his old heart beat no more.

They let him alone to work and sweat
For a wife's and children's ease.
But they hung him up for a little beer
With a woman on his knees.

STEAM SHOVEL CUT

And he might have died in bed in a year,
For when they opened him up
They found his heart was a played out pump,
And leaked like a rusty cup.

And a man can live as the church decrees,
Or dance in the way of vice,
A woman's womb is a thing of doom,
And life is the current price.

'Tis a vampire bat, or the leather box
From which you rattle the dice.
'Tis an altar of doom, is a woman's womb,
And man is the sacrifice.

THE HOUSES

You wonder why I bought so many houses,
Bought and repaired, built over home on house.
The first one was to make a home for Mary,
And Frank and Bessie, for I had myself
A settled home when I was boy and man,
And knew the feeling of respect, content
Which comes of one familiar and continued
Habitation for a boy who's growing.
The first house, then, was poor enough, God knows!
A place that smelt in all the rooms of breath
A sick man breathes into the very paper.
The rat holes in the base boards had to be
Stopped up with plaster, all the floors were loose.
Bricks lay awry upon the chimney tops.
An old well with a windlass on the porch
Made one remember typhoid all the time.
Some apple trees half-rotted, covered over
With water sprouts stood in a yard of weeds.
A barn was at the yard's end out of shape
From leaning at an angle.   All in all
The place was haunted, but it was the best
I could afford just then, and naturally
She hated it and grumbled all the time.

THE HOUSES

A few years past, it seemed scarce two or three,
And all the children married, went away.
Just then I grew more prosperous and built over
The haunted house, and built a handsome barn,
Cut out the apple trees, destroyed the weeds,
And put an iron fence around the yard.
Put bathrooms, running water in the house.
She jawed at me for doing this, and asked
Why did you wait until the children left?
Of course she knew, but blamed me just the same.
And so we had no pleasure with this house.
She wanted larger rooms, and trees in front,
A sunny dining room — there was that porch
On which ours looked, and though I closed the well
She often wondered why we had not died
Before I closed it.

           And about this time
Our banker moved away and left his house
For sale at public auction.   I went down
Alone, not telling her, to look at it.
Here was a house upon a stone foundation
Built of red brick, peaked roof of slate, three stories,
Brick walks about the yard with plots of flowers,
A barn of brick — it was the very place!
There now were grandchildren; and so I dreamed
How they would romp about this lovely yard,
Or play on rainy days in that wide garret.

THE GREAT VALLEY

And so I bid and got the house at auction.
But when I told her she was up in arms:
The house would hold a family of ten!
Besides the upper rooms were far too small:
What is a dining room, or huge drawing room
If you step out of bed against the wall?
Then there's that gully just below the barn
Breeding malaria, the banker's family
Were sick year in and out — that's why they sold it
For anything at public sale.   O fool!
Well, Mary came that summer with her children,
And my poor dream· in part was realized.
But Frank and Bessie moved to California
And never saw the happiness I planned
For them and for their children.   Mary's husband
Disliked the house — his hatred was beginning.
Next summer Mary left him and divorced him,
And started out to earn her children's bread.
She didn't come again.

                            And so it was true,
We didn't need so large a house — we sold it
And bought a cottage of six rooms; this time
She joined with me in picking out the house,
But that was nothing, for no other house
Besides this one was up for sale just then.
No sooner had we moved than she was full
Of wounded memory and a mad regret:

THE HOUSES

She saw what she had lost.   These little rooms!
This front fence almost jammed against the door!
And stoves again instead of radiators!
No running water, only an old pump
Above the kitchen sink!   And near the station —
The bawling bussmen bothered her at night!
The midnight train woke her unfailingly.
And now she said our first house was all right
With this, or that corrected.   We had blundered
In ever selling it and taking on
Such luxury in the brick house.   It had spoiled
Her taste for living in a house like this,
With just a little yard, that hideous fence,
Which one could touch while standing in the door!
She said she could not breathe because of it,
And railed against her fate so that it brought
The next step in my life of buying houses. . . .

Dreams entered in my brain of fields and woods,
A little lake perhaps, river or stream.
There was a fad of buying farms just then.
I went to Michigan on other business,
And there I saw one, bought it on the spot.
You see I had the passion as of drink,
And knew it as I ventured once again.
But then there was the house upon the bluff!
And there below it was the river! there
Beeches and oaks down to the river's edge!

THE GREAT VALLEY

A great white house all new, and apple trees,
A vineyard and a field of eighty acres.
Here will I sit, I said, upon my bluff
And watch the river.   I will keep a man
To farm the place, and prune the vines and trees,
This is the place at last.   But then I thought
What will she say?   She wants a farm I know,
But will this suit her?   So I sent for her.
And when she came she kissed me, she was glad,
Commended my good judgment, loved the house,
Went through the barn in rapture, stood beneath
The windmill, which was near, to watch it pump.
Strolled down the wooded bluff, threw pebbles in
The river where the swallows dipped and flew,
And gathered daisies by the river's shore.
I sat down in the grass flushed through with joy,
Like one who finds his haven, who has solved
Laborious troubles, thinking of the rest
I should take here — a man to run the place,
And months of summer recreation here!
I told her what my plan was.

                              No, she said,
To own a farm is business.   You should know
By this time that you have no head for business.
I think you've shown some wisdom in this farm,
Or better you've had luck in buying it.
Your other ventures buying houses were

THE HOUSES

Enough to make you have distrust of self.
Now that you've bought the farm to make it pay
Is what we have in hand, and you must work.
We'll keep a man, but he cannot do all
There is to do here, I will work and you
Must work as well, the farm must pay, you know.
I want the man to live with us in the house
So I can watch him, rout him out to work
At sun-up and keep watch upon his time.

We'll keep two rooms for our use.   For the man
Must have a family, these single fellows
Are off too much at night and think too much
In working hours of what they'll do at night.

Perhaps I am a weakling with my dream
Of buying houses, for I dream of joys
And build my palaces, invite my joys
To enter and be glad.   They never come!
She took the farm and ran it.   It was business,
But business in disorder with a loss
For seed which did not sprout, and stock that died,
And glutted markets when the fruit was good.
I worked awhile, I fished once in the river,
I sat a few times on my wooded bluff —
And then I fled and left her to the farm
To rule a single farmer who cut weeds,
Abandoned weeds for plowing, left the plow

THE GREAT VALLEY

To make a flower bed, following her whims
Obedient, indifferent to results. . . .

If you destroy a bird's nest that's the end.
The nesting birds return to find the branch
Where they had builded with such patient care,
All naked of their work.   They look and fly
And think of what?   But build no more that year.
But if you take a twig and scratch the grains
About the ant hill, overturn their work,
Stop up the door, the little folk begin
To build again, clear out the ruined hall —
They cannot be discouraged like the birds.
I think I am an ant — for even yet
I'm looking for a house, or better a home.
There is that house walled in with earth — that's
    sure —
But if there is no house to fill my joy
Why have I looked for houses all my life?

THE CHURCH AND THE HOTEL

Over the dead lake
And in a dusty sky
The full moon is speared by the spire of the Baptist
    church;
Or now it hangs over the Groveland Hotel:
I do not know whether it is over the spire
Or over the hotel.

In a dusty sky the moon
Is the bottom of a copper kettle
Which cannot be scoured into brightness.
The sky is a faded mosquito net
Over a brass cylinder cap
Dulled with verdigris.

Some years ago,
Not many years ago,
The Rev. Albert McDugall, D.D.
At the pulpit under this spire
With habitual regularity
Used to say:
Let us pray.
And the Rev. Albert McDugall, D.D.

With habitual regularity
Used to preach
On the wages of sin.
And on Sunday evenings
As he was saying let us pray,
Ed Breen in Henry Hughes' buffet,
There in the Groveland Hotel
Sitting with cronies at a table would say:
"Another round, Henry,
Bourbon for me."

And at 7:30,
At the very moment
When the Rev. Albert McDugall, D.D.
Was saying let us pray,
Ed Breen would be beginning the night,
And would be saying to Henry Hughes:
"Another round, Henry,
Bourbon for me."

You, Rev. Albert McDugall, D.D.
Lived to a ripe age.
You lived to marry a second wife.
And you, Ed Breen, died in the thirties.
But whether it be better to have ptomaine poisoning
From eating cold chicken,
Or to drug yourself to death with bourbon
I will ask the moon.

[186]

THE CHURCH AND THE HOTEL

For there is the moon
Like a German silver watch
Under a grimy show case.
I think it hangs as much over the hotel
As over the church.

SUSIE

Where did you go, pale Susie, after the day
    You left the service of the boarding house?
    The night before we made carouse
    And danced the time away.

We boys were in the kitchen and were drinking
    Small beer — you slapped the hands of us
    Who stroked your arms half amorous —
    Where did you go, I'm thinking?

Medical students up at Hahnemann
    Hunt women on a Saturday night.
    And sing, tell tales, and verse recite,
    And rush the forbidden can.

The paltry mistress made you pay for all
    The fault of us, and packed you out of doors
    When you had scrubbed the floors,
    And swept the entrance hall.

I watched you in your faded cloak and hat
    With canvas bag walk towards the Grove.
    Then something in my fancy hove,
    Laughing I caught you at

SUSIE

The doorway of the hotel on the street
    Where I had tracked you round from thirty-first.
    You laughed and cried and called me worst
    Of devils on two feet.

There I had followed you and seized you when
    You did not care what happened, so
    You fell into my hands, you know —
    'Tis twenty years since then.

I never saw you after that, nor heard
    In all this city aught of you.
    You vanished like a blot of dew,
    Or ashen hued seed bird.

I wonder if you wed a red bull-throat
    Who ran a rivet hammer, drove a truck,
    Bore many children or worse luck
    Went where the drift weeds float. . . .

HAVING HIS WAY

We parted at the Union Station,
Tom Hall and I,
Two boys in the early twenties
Fresh from the quiet of fields,
And the sleepy silence of village life.
And we stepped into Adams Street,
Noisy from trucks and rattling cars,
And babbling multitudes.
He with his great invention,
And I with my translation of Homer,
And the books of Rousseau and Marx.

And he went his way
To sell his great invention.
And I in the village glory
Of clothes ill-fitting, timid, sensitive
And proud, a little learned, so zealous
For the weal of the world
Came to your chateau palace near the Drive,
To you my friend, my queenly cousin,
For a little visit before I entered
Upon the city's life.

HAVING HIS WAY

You looked me over with calm Egyptian eyes,
And put me at ease with your lovely smile.
And there was about you the calm of desert air in
    Nevada
That made me forget myself.
Yet you began to guide me with subtlest words,
And to mould me with delicate hands,
As one might smooth a rumpled collar,
Or fasten a loosened scarf,
Or lift to place a strand of hair
Of one beloved who thrills to the touch.
Even with closed eyes you saw everything
Of harmony, or form, or hue.
There were silver strings in your little ears
Which caught the tone pictures of sounds,
And the intonations and sonorities of voices;
Which trembled to the barbarities of unmelodic words.
And there as you saw and heard me,
(I knew it at once,)
You took me for your piece of bronze in the rough
To be made under your hands
Your triumph, your work, your creation
In the world where you ruled as queen.
You would see me as finished art
Move before admiring eyes
Where music is and richness,
And where poverty and struggle
And sacrifice and failure are forgotten.

That was the cousin you meant me to be.
And in a few nights
There was an evening dress and fine linen
And an opera hat and cloak
Laid out for me in my snow white room,
And a valet came to help me.
For we were to see Carmen together —
You and I in a box.
You the queen,
And I a genius from the country
Of whom the word had gone the rounds:
A translator of Homer,
And a dreamer of revolutions,
Her cousin, you know!

I was pale from fear and pride
As I entered the box with you.
I felt I was wronging my dreams
And apostatizing all I had dreamed
To be in this box with you.
And a sullen hatred of everything:
The mass of color, the faint perfumes,
The lights, the jewels, the dazzling breasts
Of the queens in the boxes angered me.
And everyone was smiling, and everyone was leveling
Opera glasses, sometimes at me,
A translator of Homer
And a dreamer of socialism.

HAVING HIS WAY

And there like a fool I sat and thought
Of the cold without and the beggar man
Who stood at your carriage as we alighted.

And when the music arose at last
A sort of madness whirled in my brain.
For what was this Carmen thing
But subtle wickedness and cruel lust
And hardest heathenism,
And delight that seeks its own,
In a setting of bloody voluptuousness,
Fiendish caprice and faithlessness,
In music through which a pagan soul
Had sensed and voiced it all?
Till at least (I almost shrieked at this)
Don Jose in his amorous madness
Plunged a knife in the back of the whore he loved
To the growl of horns and moan of viols. . . .

And you sat through it all
Like a firefly on a vine leaf
Suspiring in all your body,
And gazing with calm Egyptian eyes,
Or turning to me as if you would know
If the poison was in my blood. . . .
But I was immune:
Democracy seemed too glorious,
And the cause of the poor too just,

THE GREAT VALLEY

And fair sweet love of men and women
So worth the cost to gain and keep,
And honest bread too sweet —
I was immune. . . .
And I scarcely saw the fair slim girl
To whom you introduced me.
And I scarcely heard what you said in the carriage
About her countless riches.
And I scarcely heard your words of praise
That I looked like a prince,
And that you meant to help me,
And do by me what your husband would do
If he were living,
And lift me along to a place in life
Where power and riches are,
And beauty is and music,
And where struggle and sacrifice are forgotten.

And when I did not answer you thought
I sat abashed by your side.
Instead in my mind were running
The notes to Queen Mab,
And bits of Greek.
I did this to stifle my wrath,
And to forget the cage you were luring me into,
And the poison you were offering me,
And the cause of Truth!
And hiding my wrath in a day or two

HAVING HIS WAY

I left you saying I would return,
But I never returned.

Instead I went where the youths were thinking,
Painting and writing,
And talking of the revolution,
And the glorious day to come.
And I was happy even though
They sent my great translation back
As poor and amateurish.
For the years of youth were long ahead
There was time to try again. . . .

Then Margaret's stepmother
Drove her from home, and she came to the city
Crying in her loneliness and destitution,
Suffering from her lame hip.
And even these were happy days,
For I loved her for her sorrows,
I loved her for her lameness.
It was all transfigured through my love
For democracy and sacrifice,
And the sweetness of honest bread.
And it was like taking the sacrament, our marriage.
And there in our little flat far out
On Robey Street I toiled at writing
While she went about so lame,
Trying to keep the house for me,

THE GREAT VALLEY

And to clear away the disorders
Which piled about her constantly
And were never cleared away. . . .

And is it not strange that to-day,
After the lapse of ten years
These two things happen within an hour?
Your letter from Rome arrived —
For though I scorned your life and love,
And went my way,
You write me still it seems,
Not to wound my fallen state,
Nor to show me what my life had been
If I had heeded you.
But just in the continuous sunshine
Of noble friendship to show me
I am sometimes in your thought.
And scarcely had your letter come
When Tom Hall crept up the creaking stairs
Dragging his feet with the help of a cane —
He is rich and came to help me.
And Tom Hall had his way as well:
He hated marriage and went the rounds,
Wherever a pretty face allured.
And now he is sick and dragging his feet.
And here am I at a writing desk:
I'm cap and bells for the Daily Globe
And my grind is a column a day.

HAVING HIS WAY

You see it comes to this, dear queen:
Can a man or woman alive escape
The granite's edges or ditch's mire,
The thorny thickets or marsh's gas,
Or the traps one thinks would never be set
Except for the fox or wolf? . . .
And here is Margaret down with a cough
Never to rise from her bed again.
And I sit by at my task of jokes,
And I stop to read your letter again,
And wonder why life has never caught you,
And why you are laughing there in Rome
Where you dine with happy friends;
Or tramp the thickets around the ruins
Of the Baths of Caracalla —
I see the platforms and dizzy arches
Under a sky of Italy.
It's cloudy here and the elevated
Rattles and roars beneath my window.
You're picking flowers while it's winter here.
I read these things in your letter and wonder
Is the asp at your breast in spite of laughter?
Or when is the asp to sting you?

THE ASP

As the train rushed on
The days of our youth swept through me,
As if they were brought to life by a sort of friction.
I thought of how madly you laughed
When we played at blindman's buff with the Miller
girls;
And of the May baskets we made together,
And hung as we rang the bell and ran.
And of our games in the first spring days
When we stole from house to house.
And the children were shouting
And the April moon was new.
And the smell of burning leaves
And the first tulips filled us with such ecstasy.
We laughed, we shouted, we leaped for joy.
We ran like mad through the rooms,
And we went to bed at last
Laughing and gasping,
And lay looking at the moon through the leafless
boughs,
And fell to sleep with joyous hearts,
Thinking of to-morrow,
And the days and days to come for play,
And the summer to come,

THE ASP

And all the mad raptures of school at an end,
And no death, and no end
Of the love of father and mother,
And the home we loved.

And here it was spring again —
But such a spring!
At the end of such years and years
And births and births and spheres and spheres of life,
Each like a life or a world of its own
With its friends, its own completeness, its rounded end.
And back of them all
Our old home forgotten,
Our father and mother gone,
And back of this spring that ended world of ours
Wherein we parted
Grown misty too!
And as the train rushed on
And the hour of meeting you neared
I was thrilled with gladness, thrilled with fear.
And now the station was Herkimer,
And now it was Amsterdam,
And now it was Albany,
And then Poughkeepsie on the Hudson.
And I looked from the car to the passing scene,
And back to the car again.
Or I turned in my seat
Or took up my book and laid it down,

Or fastened my bag for the hundredth time,
Or straightened my cloak on the seat,
And waited and waited.
For I had a story to tell you
That I could not wait to tell.
I was traveling a thousand miles to tell you,
And to get your advice, to have your solace,
To look in your eyes again,
And to feel in spite of springs that were gone,
And our old home, and father and mother gone
There was an arm in the world for me to lean on.

And the train rushed on
Bringing me nearer to you.
And the tears welled up to my eyes
As I wondered why life had mangled me so:
Why the man I loved at first and hated afterward
Had died that tragic death,
Leaving me with memories of that love,
And such agony for that hate.
And why as a sort of Empress Eugenia
The world turned on me when I fell,
And the little power I had departed.
And why in spite of my aspiration
I had run into such disgust,
Such overthrow of my work,
Such undoing of myself,
Such spiritual wreck and shame!

THE ASP

And to think of what had done it:
My search for love, my struggle for excellence —
These things alone!
I had married this second man for love,
And because I believed in him
As a man of power, a man of thought,
A man who loved me.
And hoping through him to retrieve my life
From the smut of the man I married first.
But I found my very soul deceived:
He was just a violent visionary,
A frothing fool,
A spendthrift, coward, hedonist.
And there I was tied to him.
And carrying his child while finding him out.
So I used to stand with my face to the wall
And choke my mouth with a handkerchief
To keep from crying out.
For I knew if a whimper passed my lips
I should fall and roll on the floor with madness,
And beat my head on the floor.

So when the train rolled into the station
A sickness, a weakness came over me.
I had spent myself in expectation.
And now that I was about to see you,
The thought of the vainness of seeing you,
And the thought that you could not help me,

THE GREAT VALLEY

Though I had traveled these thousand miles,
Made me wish to fly, to hide.
So I stepped from the train in a kind of daze,
And scarcely felt your kiss.
It seemed relaxed, so faint.
And your voice was weak.
And your eyes were dim and dry.

And there in the cab as we drove to the Park
I was still in a daze
Talking of May baskets
And blindman's buff,
And laughing, for one always laughs
When the moment is worst.
And so it was I did not really see you.
But when we began to walk
Things about you began to limn themselves:
Your shoulders seemed a little bent.
There were streaks of snow on your temples.
And you were quiet with the terrible quietness
Of understanding of life.
And the old wit I knew,
And the glad defiance of fate,
And the light in your eyes,
And the musical laugh
All were gone.
Perhaps the daily grind of Cap and Bells
Had sapped you, dear.

THE ASP

But when I looked at your hand on your cane
And saw how white and slim it was,
And how it trembled, I knew
You were not the giant man of old,
Though you said you were gaining strength again,
And I could lean on your arm.

Well, then I told you all:
How my search for love had fooled me again;
And how this beast had wronged and robbed me;
And how he stood in his paranoiac rages,
And compared himself to Christ.
But when I began to speak of the child,
What a darling girl she was,
You sank in a seat and said: "No more —
I didn't think I was weak as this —
You mustn't tell me another thing,
Not now, not just now."
Then I saw, what Time had done,
And I saw that you could not help me.
And the next day and the next day,
When I did not see you,
And weeks passed by and I scarcely saw you,
And I scarcely saw you again,
Though I had come a thousand miles
To lean on your arm,
It grew in my mind that you despised me,
Or that you were indifferent to my lot,

THE GREAT VALLEY

Or at least that I was a wounded thing
You could not bear to see.
Till at last, though I knew
That my way was clear: there was nothing to do
But to fly with my child,
And leave him forever,
And endure great loneliness forever, if need be,
And whatever shame there was,
For the sake of my soul's honor,
Which only myself could save,
And you could save not at all.
Though I knew, I say, that my way was clear,
And I needed your help not at all,
Still in a kind of madness
I began to reproach you for not helping me,
And for abandoning me to my fate.
As a sick child will cry and blame its mother
When it is not healed at once.

And that was the mood he found me in
When he came with a smile and honey words.
Well, I fell in his arms, and here I am
Plunged up to the mouth in spiritual muck,
And what life is left for me now?
How can I go on with life?
For he hates me now as a humbled thing,
He has broken my pride and he hates me now.
And he roars and curses about the house,

THE ASP

And yells at our little girl when she cries,
And stands with his hands outstretched and says
That his fate is worse than Christ's.
And I tremble and rustle around like a fallen leaf,
And neither laugh nor cry nor return him a word. . . .

For you know there's a spring,
And you know there's a fire,
To burn dead leaves.
And after the ashes
There's a spirit given a chance!

THE FAMILY

We were three larks in the same nest.
All spring the wind blew from the west.
We chirped beneath the enshadowing wheat,
It grew to green, it grew to gold.
Our mother's voice was piercing sweet
To see how strong we were and bold —
How palpitant of wing.

We knew our father not, alas!
A hunter slew him while the grass
Was fresh beneath the April rain.
And ere I had the strength to fly
Our brother sang a farewell strain
And soared into the empty sky.
And then our sister knew the fear
And hunger of a serpent's eye.
And our sweet mother, lone and drear,
Fled far afield and left me here
To nurse my heart and sing.

THE SUBWAY

There was the white face of Fear,
And the solemn face of Duty,
And the face of self looking in the mirror.
But there were voices calling from vernal hilltops,
And silver spirits by moonlit gardens calling,
And voices of no sound from far horizons calling,
But even if there be penitence for living
And thought and tears for the past
And even shame and even hunger;
And if there be nothing gained at the last in living,
And much to pay for the madness of briefest bliss;
And if there be nothing in life, and life be nothing
So that to nail one's self to the cross is nothing lost —
Is Death not even less?

These were the voices whereto we tore our flower
Petal by petal apart and scattered it,
And paused and paltered.

But lest the whispers grow louder,
And the eyebrows arch to a fiercer scorn,
You fled away to France and left me
With only a poor half uttered farewell,

THE GREAT VALLEY

A scrawl put off to the last, then written
As with shut eyes, swift nervous hands:
As one might wait for the heroic thought
To take his poison — wait in vain, and then
Cowardly gulp it down and reel to death.
I could not hate you for the pain of hate,
And could not love you who had hid yourself,
Belied yourself behind this scrawl.
I could only sit half-numb,
And drift in thought.

And afterwards it wasn't so much to be alone,
Nor to dream of the days that were done,
Save as it deepened the surge in my heart,
Or strengthened the ebb of my soul for thought
Of your soul drawn away from me,
So needlessly drawn it seemed.
And it's the music that deepens and changes, —
For as your soul adds strings to its strings
There are fingers to play — it almost seems
There are fingers about us that watch and wait
For a soul that's adding strings to its harp
To play them when they're strung.
And so it's the music that deepens and changes
That kills you at last I think.

Well, I had a dream one night
That a dead man well could dream:

THE SUBWAY

They had buried me in Rosehill.
And after twenty years from France they brought you
And put you just across the walk from me
Where we slept while the crowding city grew
To a vast six millions, and they were building
A subway to Lake Forest.
And we were forgotten of everyone, ˙
And almost our family names were lost.
And our love you fled from all forgotten,
And everything we said, or thought, or felt forgotten
With the whispers of boys and girls
In a temple's shadow in Babylon.

Well, to pursue, it's a day in March
When the colors are brilliantly white and blue;
And it's cold except for Poles and Italians
Who dig with spades and cut with picks.
And some of these fellows are digging us up,
We lie in the way of the subway, you know.
And they dump our bones in a careless heap,
The ribs of me by the ribs of you,
My skull lies ignorant by your skull.
And behold our poor arms are entwined.
For death you know is a mocker of Life.
And there we lie like stocks and stones,
And where is our love and where is your fear?
And a young Pole pushes our bones together
With a lusty shove of his heavy shoe,

And he says to another: "You saw that girl
I was dancing with last night?
Well, I don't think I'm the only one.
And besides she bothers me most to death.
And as soon as this subway job is over,
Which will be in a year, or year and a half,
I'm going to beat it back to Poland."
Then the other beginning to shovel muttered:
"1976."

THE RADICAL'S MESSAGE

To the archangels and the fiery seed
Of mad Prometheus, fighting gods for men,
And heaven for earth, this greeting:
I led you once, I taught you, am the sire
Of hosts of you, but fellow to you all.
And when I fell, was chained upon this bed
By adamantine sickness, then I lay
And had you in my thought hour after hour,
Day after day, and saw you in dreams by night
Still fighting, bleeding, caring for the fallen,
Or objurgating heaven for the curse
It sheds on men, or arming for the fray
With steel of resisting thought; and so the sense
Of my responsibility has weighed
Upon me as my night has deftly dawned
To something clearer than the soul you knew,
Who led you once, with breath of iron horns,
Called to you: Charge! there is the trench of greed!
Avenge the poor! bring justice! purge the state
Of fraud! And so I lay and thought of you
Still guarding the old lines, fighting the old fights,
While I was changed, was not your leader now,
Cared no more for your battles, save as strife

THE GREAT VALLEY

That leads up higher, for upon my wall
I woke to see these words : He only wins
His freedom and existence who each day
Conquers them newly.   How can I tell you
What has come over me ?

                                    You walk through galleries,
Devour the pictures in the different rooms,
Then gaze about you where you stand at last
Amid supernal canvases of light.
Try to recall the pictures you have studied,
What you have seen has helped you to perceive
The final beauties, but is blurred in mind,
It has been lived, has lost its vital power,
Is not the sovereign moment.

                                    Climb a mountain
The whole day through, and at the time of stars
Stand on a peak and search infinity !
You have forgot the valleys, save perhaps
The torment of the flies of which you're freed
In these cool heights.

                    ───── So age cannot recall
The thrill and intimate complexities
That made the thought of youth.   A sickness comes :
One has been metamorphosed, cannot live
The old emotions, habits, old delights.

THE RADICAL'S MESSAGE

And as for that we change each day and all
Our yesterdays are chrysalises whence
We crawled to what we are.   In short, archangels,
I have become another soul.   Now listen:

I have seen things I cannot tell you of.
I have gained understandings past my power
To give you clearly; yet upon me rests
The teasing call to tell you, here I lie
Revolving this new task of leadership.
How shall I make you see I have not failed you?
Not really played a treasonous soul to you?
Not scorned the cause I gave you, kept you in?
Or damned you for, or made you suffer for?
I railed at heaven, I instructed you
To rail as well.   How can you understand
I now accept the fate?   Will you despise me
For saying this?   Or will you say disease
Has weakened me, cooled off the fire of soul
And damped my courage?   Then go on your way
To find a worthier leader?

                              So to doubt
I taught you once, but now my mind believes.
And to deny the order of the world
I gave you words, now I affirm the plan.
To fight against the gods in man's behalf,
I made my leadership.   Now I perceive

THE GREAT VALLEY

The cause of gods and men made one.   You see
It is not individual gain that counts
In these external benefits of freedom
And satisfaction of material wants,
That counts so much, I say, as inner chains
Struck from the wrists, and inner scales peeled off
From inner eyes.   I grant the human cause,
And say this, — Can I make you understand?
To give you proof my heart is with you yet
Let me reveal my sacrifice.

        Suppose
You've found a truth that others knew before you,
Seen, let us say, the cat, as single taxers
Are wont to say?   You hunt up some adherent
Who's labored with you, tell him, "I'm convinced,
I see the cat at last."   You want to share
Your joy with some one, want his dragging hope
To hear you have arrived.   And so with me
I hungered to communicate my vision
To some one who had seen it, and who knew
Its meaning, what it meant to me.

        But then
You archangels and hot Promethean seed
Each time I thought of making the confession
To some delighted spirit, ranged yourselves
In thought around my sick bed, with contempt,

Or pained compassion written on your brows,
And words like these: He has deserted us,
He has surrendered, cringed before the gods.
And so my sacrifice is this: You'll be
The first to know my second birth, you can
In such case never charge it up to fear,
Or weakness, shrunken nerves, or spirit
That lost the human touch through the effects
Of some delirium.   What mind so clear,
Or will so strong to die with this denial
For your sakes?   For it may be best for you
To live the rebel out of you.   And if
You thought — at least I fear it — if you thought
I had gone over to the hosts you hate,
As you are now, through weakness, made my peace
With heaven, as you'd call it, just to save
My wretched self, you'd have a mad regret,
A fine disgust to work through, added labor
To all you must achieve.   That's why I die,
And seal this message.   Break it on the day
They make me ashes!

BOMBYX

Sealed in a cocoon-cradle of white silk,
Locked fast in sleep;
Or bound for years as a chrysalid, while the neap
Creative tides rise to the spring and slough
The torn strands and the golden pupa stuff,
You tear wings free for the connubial flight —
Break suddenly the embryo trance, drift off,
Whole troops of you in a looped and colorful clutter
Wobbling like leaves in a fresh wind's delight.
And over clover meadows in a flutter,
Or through sweet scented hollows,
You seek the expectant mate,
And the mad moment where life turns to death,
And both become one essence and one breath,
One undivided fate.

Together you fly
Drunken with life, yet mad to die,
Since soul achievement is death after all,
All rivals for the wedding festival.
Yet only one of you can win the prize;
The rest shall sink exhausted in defeat,
While the triumphant bridegroom dies
In his own rapture and creative fire —
All perish in the flame of their desire.

BOMBYX

For none of you is given strength to live
Beyond the quest, or the hymeneal kiss;
The disappointed perish
One wins his joy, but may not keep or cherish
The moment which contains it, sudden doom
Falls on the winner of his bliss
And on the wings that quiver their frustration.

Bombyx! to have more life than is enough
To win the mate, achieve the one success,
And on that life to mount and half survey
The universe —
Build cities with it, letter precious scrolls,
Plan for the race to be and have the vision
To labor for of ages half elysian,
Is that a benediction or a curse?
Is it a good or evil to have strength
To soar beyond the sun, or planets even
If none of us at length
Reach heaven?
If none of our infatuate souls
Sip the bright fire of God?
If it be all a flying in a dream,
A lying down at last in deeper night,
To enrich the prodigal sod,
To breed new wings
For the same flight?

THE APOLOGY OF DEMETRIUS

Hyacinthus, your money, the idol you ordered is
 finished.
May the grace of Diana be with you in strength un-
 diminished.

Behold how the breast of it glitters, as if it were
 wrought in with stipples.
The Ephesian goddess is nature and these are her
 bountiful nipples.

So then do I fear for my trade? No, never! It's
 past my conceiving.
There'll be work for the artist while gods change to
 win our believing.

Come on then, you babblers and madmen from Jewry
 and tell us and show us —
Yes, come with your tumult the like of which never
 was known in Corinth or Troas.

They crowd in the markets and temples and gabble a
 story that palters.
Well, I whistle and hammer the silver, a maker of
 statues and altars.

[218]

THE APOLOGY OF DEMETRIUS

Who says I am wroth lest in Samothrace, Lystra and
    Delos
The craft of the maker of images fail through the
    speech of these fellows?

And the temple of Artemis perish?   Oh, well, however
    they hate us
Can they burn it as once it was burned by the wretch
    Herostratus?

But we built it again and carved it all newly in beauty
    and wonder —
Destroy it, oh man, who was crazed by lightning and
    roaring of thunder!

Oh virgin Diana, if virgin, what virgin whose altar is
    older!
If matron what breasts hang with milk for the eyes of
    her temples' beholder!

For centuries gone — when these Jews prayed to ser-
    pents of bronze and calves that were golden
In Ephesus, Arcady, Athens, our reverent love was
    beholden

To the goddess of prophecy, music, the lyre, of light,
    inspiration,
Who guarded and watches the city and lays the foun-
    dation

Of nations and laws. What works we have done, yea
    still we would heed her —
And look at your barbarous ark in your temple of jewels
    and cedar!

What is our pollution, our idols, our sacrificed things
    which are strangled?
I ask you already divided in turbulent parties who
    wrangled

Concerning salvation of God to the faith of the uncir-
    cumcision
In Cyprus and Paphos, where poets of love keep the
    Hellenic vision.

I am filled with my loathing! Oh keep me a Greek
    though you make me a whoreson,
When the worship of beauty is dead you may pare off
    my foreskin.

When the symbol is dead which I mould to Diana our
    goddess
I'll retire to the country of Nod, no matter where Nod
    is.

It will live when your temples are built, if any are
    builded,
And Jesus in silver is nailed on a cross which is gilded.

THE APOLOGY OF DEMETRIUS

And touching this thing is it different to worship a
    man or abstraction?
Or an idol of silver or stone? — go talk to your spirit's
    distraction!

Areopagus listened to Paul, I am told, for Athens is
    spending
Her time, as of old, in weighing new things and at-
    tending.

They heard him in silence! Let his arguments pass
    uncorrected —
Why, Plato had told us of Er from the dead resur-
    rected!

Now, mark me! For showing the wisdom, compas-
    sion of poets and sages
That silence like lightning will aureole Paul to the end
    of the ages.

Oh Athens, who set up that shrine, do you think it was
    just superstition
Which carved for all passers to see that profoundest
    inscription:

To the unknown God? Do you think it was cowardice
    even?
Make altars and gods as you will, unknown is the
    planeted heaven.

And we who are richest in gods — have exhausted all
    thought in creating
Both symbols and shapes for interpreted loving and
    hating

Still sense the Unknown, though in blindness, in love
    as in duty
Would worship it most — the Unknown is the ultimate
    beauty.

Yes, Athens who set up the altar and chiseled the wor-
    shipful letters
To the Unknown God — what ignorance fastened with
    fetters

Did you loosen, oh wonder of Tarsus, how help their
    unknowing
Who told them he dwelt not in temples, nor needed
    the flowing

Of prayers from men's hearts — the Giver of life and
    of all things, and seeing
He is lord of the heavens, in whom we are living and
    having our being.

So quoting our poet who centuries since with the mon-
    arch Gonatas
Lived and wrote the Phaenomena, known to the
    Greeks as Aratus.

THE APOLOGY OF DEMETRIUS

And yet Hyacinthus I pity this Paul for profoundest
    compassion
Of Jesus before him. This sky and this earth I can
    fashion

Through mystical wonder or fear to the Sphinx or the
    Minotaur dreaded.
There's Persephone dying and rising, and Cerberus the
    dog many-headed.

We have thought it all through! Yet I say if a virtue
    Elysian
Resides in the doctrine I'll leave off the goddess
    Ephesian;

Sell my tools, shut my shop, worship God in a way
    that is safer,
Make the Unknown the known! Have they shown
    you a magical wafer?

A PLAY IN FOUR ACTS

Act One

There was slight rain that afternoon,
And tempest in the apple trees;
But as the sun went down the moon
Sailed swiftly to a western breeze.

Day kindled something in your blood,
Your fancies roved with dove and hawk;
There was no promise in your mood
Nor soft assurance in your talk.

I felt you might mislead my trust
And slight a love too surely yours;
You were so wild, I felt you must
Be kindred to the woods and moors.

But when we passed the orchard through
The dusk had crept into the sky;
Your eyes betrayed a dream which grew
Until I thought I heard you sigh.

You were an ardent star that waited
For night to be yourself and show

A PLAY IN FOUR ACTS

How surely afternoon had fated
A love that nothing could forego.

Act Two

The sky was full of clouds at rest
Like dolphins in a waste of blue.
We tramped along a country road
Into the village, I and you.

The dogwood bloomed along the fences.
We heard the songs of larks and thrushes.
The country door-yards teemed with hues
Of lilac trees and almond bushes.

The long blaze of the setting sun
Shone in your eyes and analyzed
Their little rifts of gray and brown,
And left your secret undisguised.

And I was silent thinking over
The old threads raveled from your heart.
I hear you clearer now than then:
"How can we part? How can we part?"

Act Three

Shadows upon the wall
And the ghost of a past on the floor,
Here where the hours made carnival
In the days that are no more.

THE GREAT VALLEY

And the chamber is cold and bare,
And the wax from the taper drips;
But I bury my face in your hair,
And swoon at the touch of your lips.

We went from the house to the wood,
But never a word we spoke;
And an eerie wind like our mood
Rustled the leaves of the oak.

Dead leaves, tremulous, crisp,
That breathed a forgotten tune;
A cloud the shape of a wisp
Blotted the soaring moon.

Silent we walked the path,
And then the wild farewell;
I saw your form like a wraith
Fade in the forest's dell.

If joy would never depart,
If we could but still the pain —
Dear, I awoke with a pang in my heart
And heard the sound of the rain.

Act Four

Michigan Avenue streams with people —
Ten years alter the avenue.
It's April again, and there are dolphin
Clouds at rest in a waste of blue.

A PLAY IN FOUR ACTS

A girl goes by with a spray of lilacs
Pinned at her breast, and quick as thought
Country fences, dogwood blossoms
Over the granite scene are wrought.

You come in my mind! It's spoiled by the glimpse
Of a monster diamond that glints and glows;
A black-eyed Gadarene goes past
Insolent, heavy, and hooked of nose.

I scan his face that runs with fat,
And the fleshly sag of his under lip;
Then back to the diamond again, the hand
Holds your arm with a master grip!

THEODORE DREISER

Jack o' Lantern tall shouldered,
One eye set higher than the other,
Mouth cut like a scallop in a pie,
Aslant showing powerful teeth.
Swaying above the heads of others.
Jubilant with fixed eyes, scarcely sparkling.
Moving about rhythmically, exploding in laughter.
Touching fingers together back and forth,
Or toying with a handkerchief.
And the eyes burn like a flame at the end of a funnel.
And the ruddy face glows like a pumpkin
On Halloween!

Or else a gargoyle of bronze
Turning suddenly to life
And slipping suddenly down corners of stone
To eat you:
Full of questions, objections,
Distinctions, instances.
Contemptuous, ironical, remote,
Cloudy, irreverent, ferocious,
Fearless, grim, compassionate, yet hateful,

THEODORE DREISER

Old, yet young, wise but virginal.
To whom everything is new and strange:
Whence he stares and wonders,
Laughs, mocks, curses.
Disordered, yet with a passion for order
And classification — hence the habitual
Folding into squares of a handkerchief.

Or else a well cultivated and fruitful valley,
But behind it unexplored fastnesses,
Gorges, precipices, and heights
Over which thunder clouds hang,
From which lightning falls,
Stirring up terrible shapes of prey
That slink about in the blackness.
The silence of him is terrifying
As if you sat before the sphinx.
The look of his eyes makes tubes of the air
Through which you are magnified and analyzed.
He needs nothing of you and wants nothing.
He is alone, but content,
Self-mastered and beyond friendship,
You could not hurt him.
If he would allow himself to have a friend
He could part from that friend forever
And in a moment be lost in wonder
Staring at a carved rooster on a doorstep,
Or at an Italian woman

THE GREAT VALLEY

Giving suck to a child
On a seat in Washington Square.

Soul enwrapped demi-urge
Walking the earth,
Stalking Life !

JOHN COWPER POWYS

Astronomer and biologist
And chemical analyst and microscopist,
Observer of men's involuted shells
Where they conceal their hate and even their love
Under insipid ooze or nacreous stuff.
Tracer of criss-cross steps made when great hells
Kept lime as soft as wax
Which thereupon took the imprint of the air
From gnat-like wings of joy or shadowy care.
He makes hard secrets stand in the cul de sac's
Entrance and face him till he lays all bare
That eyes hold or heart of blood contains,
And curious traits in diverse curious brains,
And starved desires in hearts and hopes forgot
Under the sifting ashes of one's lot.

X-ray photographer who flashes
What's in you out of you with sudden crashes
Of wit or oratory in a flood.
He samples and tests the book's, also your blood.
Shows what you are and whence you came,
And who your kindred are, and what your flame
In heat and color is.   Poet and wag,

THE GREAT VALLEY

Prophet, magician taking from a bag
Eggs, rabbits, silver globes; the old engram!
Scoffer with reverence, visioned, quick to damn,
Yet laugh at, looking keenly through the sham.
Confessing his own sins, devoid of shame.
He knows himself and laughs,
Or blames himself as he would others blame.
A naughty boy who kicks away the staff
Which poor decrepits walk by, nearly blind,
Then hurrying up with varied thought to find
Medicinal clay with which dim eyes to heal.

What is the human secret but Proteus'?
And who can catch the old man but his kind? .
He was Poseidon's herdsman, knew the streams
Of early being, sea-filled ponds and sluices,
Where life took birth through elemental dreams.
And Proteus glanced with lightning and divined
The cause of Bacchus' madness.   But at noon
He counted his sea-calves and ocean-sheep
On Carpathos where waters made a tune
Following the Orphic sun out of the deep —
Then in his cave he hid him, turned to sleep. . . .

So runs our life to change! and who can catch
The Protean thought must watch,
And be adept at wrestling, in the chase.
And know the god whatever be his face,

JOHN COWPER POWYS

Through roar of water where the porpoises
And extravagant dolphins play, in silences
Of noon or midnight.   So John Cowper Powys
You stand before us gesturing, shoulder bent
A little like King Richard, frizzed of hair,
Rolling your eye for secrets, for the word.
The thresher of your mind is eloquent
With hulls and flakes of words, until at last
The kernel itself pops out, not long deferred. . . .

Here is our wrestler then,
Hunter of secrets of creative souls.
Eluded he may be, he tries again.
His hand slips clutching at the irised shoals
Of rapturous thought.   And at times his eyes
Are blinded by a light, or a disguise.
But finally both eye and hand
Obey the infallible senses' brave command —
He catches Proteus then, and with a shout,
The god shouts too, and we who watch the bout
Join in the panic of their merriment!

NEW YEAR'S DAY

She was a woman who even as a child
Hungered for gifts with hunger passionate
And in her childhood made a hard fate
For a father who had failed and who was wild
With a kind of laughing despair,
That comes of having failed.
She had plain dresses, only a little strand
Of coral beads, and ribbons for her hair
Bestowed by grandmama.   And on her hand
A ring of beads that maddened her and paled
Beside the gold rings other girls could show.
So she grew up out of this woe
Of wanting and not having things.
And round this nucleus of desire
Her nature wound itself into a spire,
As a vine climbs up and clings
Till it becomes the tree;
So she became all fire
For the world's glittering glory.

Then in the process of her being's story
She married a man of riches and took over
Dresses and jewels, houses, with her lover.

NEW YEAR'S DAY

And learned the ways of Paris and New York,
And how to sit, or look, or use one's fork.
And how to speak in French, and how to dress.
And how to find and use the loveliness
That gold brings. And she lived where thought is
    white
With its great longing for the infinite,
Where pale youths dream and write,
And starve and lie awake at night;
Where sculpture, music and where painting is
On priceless canvases.
But none of this saw she
In feeding her desire with jollity
In the cafés and in society;
Wherever the denials of her youth
Could be made whole, or leveled up
With idle splendor or the champagne cup.
That was her dream of making her life truth,
Till she devoured her husband like a leman —
She was at last one of this kind of women.
Then as a widow she came journeying back
With trunks and maids upon a New Year's day
Over her childhood's disappointed track.

Her father meanwhile had gone on the way
Which was his at the start.
His life was like a bruise which does not smart
Now that it has grown hard.

And he was stoical like one who hugs
His inner self until sensation dies,
Or dulls his fears or sorrows with strong drugs.
There was a light of hardness in his eyes
Through which no one could see his secret pain.
Failure had made him so — he could explain
To no one how he had been caught in life;
Sometimes it seemed himself, sometimes his wife,
And he had thought of it so much he lost
Perspective of himself, therefore he kept
Great silence, speaking little, even then
But trivial things.   He trod his path and slept,
And rose to tread the path and slept again.
He was resolved to pay the bitter cost
And not cry out — his thinking stood on guard
To this end chiefly.

                With impassive heart
He wrote his daughter on a postal card
To come, if it should please her, and be home
On Christmas, if she could, on New Year's day
If she preferred, but anyway to come.

If a ghost could patch its tomb
With a trowel from time to time,
If it had a little lime,
So as to stop the cracks and growing rifts,
That would be like this man who hated gifts

[236]

NEW YEAR'S DAY

Because he scarce could give them, and had patched
With hardness where his heart had broken
In years gone for the holidays when she
Cried in such ignorance of his poverty.
Now with walled feelings he could sit unspoken
Of what he felt, regretted, or had lost —
He was that kind of ghost.
So when the daughter came he only had
Her mother and the dinner, greetings glad,
And certain pride because her life had matched
With childhood's hopes — but still he had no gifts
For Christmas or for New Year's, and the daughter
Wept when she found it so, — 'twas always so, —
It made her youthful bitterness alive.
And so she spilled her water
Out of a trembling hand at dinner and arose
And left the table.   But with specs on nose
Self-mastered, not revealing
What was his feeling,
The father ate the dinner alone, while mother
Was comforting the daughter.

"He might have given me a dollar, a little book,
A handkerchief, or any other
Little thing, he always acted so."
The mother tried to soothe her daughter's woe.
But while they were together, the father took
His steps up town and when the two came back

They found him gone and the room growing black
From falling night. . . .

                    But later he came in
And sat by the fire all silent. This had been
His New Year's day! And later his wife came
And sat across him silent in her blame
Of him and of his life.

                    She said at last:
"Blanche is heart sick."

                    "Well, I am sixty-five,"
He answered her, "and never while I'm alive
Will I remember Christmas or a New Year's day.
I'm glad so many of such days are past,
They have been always this way. We had dinner
And ourselves for her and she brought herself
And nothing else. This is the way to win her
Admiration, yet this thing of giving
Dollars or books, wins only a little thrill
Of tickled pride or egotism, still
I might have done it, just to have the peace
Of her self-satisfaction."

                    Said the wife:
"You might find happiness in her happiness.
The only thing you understand in living

NEW YEAR'S DAY

Is how to stand your misery, one can guess
The working of your thought."

                                    Ere she could cease
The daughter entered like the devil's elf,
And saw her father bent before the fire,
And saw the back of his head which spoke to her
Of hardness, or of something that she hated
Which moved her pity and her hate at once.

And then the mother said: "You two are fated
To be as blind as two cliffs to each other.
You need I think a spiritual re-birth,
Something that you could have upon this earth.
For I can see a book or handkerchief
Would give one happiness and one relief
From hardness which is girding in your soul.
That would be rich return for small outlay,
God give us all another New Year's day."

PLAYING BLIND

You used to play at being blind —
Now you are blind — you used to say:
"Play I am blind and help me find
Where the gate opens on the way."

I laughed at you, we laughed together
When you were playing blind, your staff
My walking cane of varnished leather —
Now you are blind and still you laugh.

You sit beneath the reading lamp
With long lashed eyelids closed and pale
And make me read you Riley's Tramp,
And Grimm and many a fairy tale.

Sometimes I stop — you see I choke
Before the tale is done by half —
One's eyes blur from tobacco smoke —
I cannot laugh now when you laugh.

I SHALL NEVER SEE YOU AGAIN

If I could only see you again —
If I could only see you again!
How can it be
I shall never see you again?
For the world has shown it can roll on its way
And blot you out forever —
And I shall never see you again!
I thrill as one who slips on the edge of a gulf
When I think I shall never see you again!

As a dead leaf is hurtled over the tops of trees;
As a dead leaf is dizzily driven through woodland
    valleys
I am driven and tossed in the storms of living.
But as the dead leaf escapes the breeze's fingers,
And sinks till it nestles motionless under a rock
So in quiet moments I dream
Of you,
I dream of all that you were —
And I shall never see you again!

There never was any one like you!
There never yet was such joy in a heart,

THE GREAT VALLEY

Such strength to live whatever the fate,
Such love to love,
Such thought to see how life is good,
Such maternal passion,
Such breasts eager to nurse child after child —
And I shall never see you again!

Your breasts were made to suckle conquerors,
Warriors, prophets,
Invincible souls
Loving life, and loving death at last.
And now your breasts are dust,
You are all dust,
You are lost save for my memory.

And this morning I woke
As a leaf might wake in its sheltered place
Under the rock
Stirred by a breath of April.
And I lived again the last time I saw you —
The last visit!
You were almost ninety then.
But there was the old zest in your heart
To do all things and have all things
Unchanged, as I had known them
As a boy.
You gave me the same room,
Nothing was changed,

I SHALL NEVER SEE YOU AGAIN

Not a chair, a curtain, a picture.
And you came up-stairs before it was day
And lighted a fire in the little stove
To have the room warm for me to dress in —
There never was love like yours!

And I went down to the kitchen and found you
Frying batter cakes, and laughing,
And bringing back my boyhood days
With the old stories.
And how you kissed me, and hugged me
With your withered arms!
And then you sat down with me,
And ate with me as of old,
And brought out priceless jars of things
Which you had made and saved for me!

The breath of memory stirs me
Under the rock.
I must have the madness of life to drive me,
To toss me
Into forgetfulness of my loss of you —
For I shall never see you again!

ELIZABETH TO MONSIEUR D——

I pace the rooms and wait for John's return.
My heart beats all too fast, I feel a pain
Around my heart, my hands grow cold, I burn
Through neck and cheeks.   And thus I live in vain.
John comes at last and says, "There is no mail,
No letter for you."   And with whirling brain
I turn away in silence, growing pale,
And whisper to myself: to be resigned
To wretchedness perhaps is to prevail
O'er wretchedness and win a peace of mind.
To love you so, to thirst for you, to pay
For outward calm with inner storms confined,
To lie awake by night and spend the day
In restless thoughts, is life too hard to bear.
I see you in my troubled dreams alway,
You face me with a grave and haughty air,
Serene, incensed against me who intrude
An interest which you have no heart to share.
Forgive me then my sorrow's servitude,
To write to you my suffering will ease,
And fill the aching of my solitude.
I have gone forth to Nature to find peace:

ELIZABETH TO MONSIEUR D——

The woods are filled with purple lupine now,
Small yellow asters, phlox, and cramoisies
Of columbine and roses, vine and bough.
The wild grape and the cherry haunt the dunes
With odors sweet as love.   To cool my brow
I walk the heights upon these afternoons
And watch the blue waste of the sky's descent.
And yesterday where golden light festoons
With flickering sorcery the way we went
'Twixt sprays of beech and sassafras I stole
Till once again at the hill's top half-spent
I saw the shore dunes and the waters roll.
We climbed it once together — it was there
The Bacchic madness came into your soul
To take me in your arms.   And now I bear
Your coldness, your reproaches, you who call
My longing and my spiritual despair
A mere neurosis, or hysterical
Outcropping to be conquered.   It was wrong
To take me in your arms, and then when all
Was not yours then to tell me to be strong,
And urge your marriage vows now I have thought
The problem of my love through.   I belong
To you Monsieur; whatever grief is wrought
Of body or of soul to satisfy
The flame is better, and is far less fraught
With mad regret than it can be to lie
In restless torture.   O my friend withdraw

Your friendship from me never lest I die!
Yes, I could live and work if I foresaw
Your friendship mine and letters by your hand
Arriving in this lonely place to thaw
The ice around my heart's flame.   Understand
From those I love but little love I need:
Crumbs from your feast you scarce can countermand,
And crumbs are all I ask, and just the meed
Of friendly interest.   I abase my pride.
The strong can suffer silently and bleed
As long as strength lasts, keep the blood inside,
Until one weakens when it spurts and drips.
And Pride turns Nature, careless now to hide
The inner bleeding bubbling at the lips.
I write you this without regret or shame.
My strength has left me in the blue eclipse
Of agony.   Monsieur, I take the blame,
If any come, of fanning dangerously
The spark that brightened once and would be flame —
Is that not true?   Or do you say to me:
"You are no more my pupil, I retrench
"The memory of things that cease to be,
"And go my way with teaching young girls French,
"As I taught you.   Two years have passed since then.
"What is this thought that time has failed to quench?
"You who are laureled in the world of men,
"A genius risen like a morning star,
"Does not that glory fill you?"   Yet again

ELIZABETH TO MONSIEUR D——

I answer you one's genius burns afar
In useless splendor if it warm no cheek,
Make bright no eye, lead on no darkling spar —
Genius is love, is freedom, it must speak,
Work out its fate from egocentric life;
It is more swift than other feet to seek
Its ruin with its hope, or take the knife
More willingly to breast than those who sink
In involuted growth.   To be your wife
I do not dream, I only wish to drink
The cup with you and break the bread with you,
To feel thereby our lives are one and think
We are one creed and one communion, new
In spirit, born anew, that I may have
An altar for my genius, something true
And near in flesh to triumph for, or brave
The world or evil for.   Genius is love.
It cannot bear itself alone to save;
It must another rescue, it must prove
Its growing strength in ministry.   Monsieur,
Bruise not my soul by ignorance hereof,
My reverend father thinks my thoughts are pure —
If he should read this!   But if you dismiss
This letter with a smile and say her cure
Is the reaction of forbidden bliss,
It is most true, but you would not degrade
My love for you with that analysis,
And that alone.   For surely God who made

THE GREAT VALLEY

Our souls and bodies so meant we should rise
Through their desires, and does God pervade
This glowing mass of life, these starry skies
With other power? Now scorn me, if you will.
The unburdened heart has tamed its agonies.

MONSIEUR D—— TO THE PSYCHOANALYST

In time I'll tell you all the dreams I've had —
But now — well, let me think! O yes three times
I've dreamed a creature with a dragon's head,
Which was her head as well, for so it seemed,
Gemmed with her brazen eyes half luminous
And half opaque, slate colored, lay across
My breast and hurt my heart, and breathed her breath
From half-dead, livid overlapping lips
(As when you crush a snake's head jaws will lie
Awry and out of plumb) like pestilence
Right in my nostrils. This interpreted
Means characters are breaths, and most are bad
When closely known. Such breath suits well the
        dragon,
But would not suit her, so you'd think to see
How fair her face, how seeming fair her soul.
So let me tell you.

                        All my hair is gray,
My youth is gone, pretense will work no more.
I'm fifty-seven, yet I cling to youth,
Because I cling to love, have never known
Aught but successions of immoderate — what?

THE GREAT VALLEY

Some call it lust — you call it libido.
Well it is urge, creative fire and drives
The artist half-soul mad, as I am mad —
Look how my poor hand trembles, my voice breaks —
No! I'll go on. I'll tell you all, be done.
Then if you cannot cure me, there's a balm
I know myself.

        If I had only loved
Elizabeth, who wrote me years ago
Such pleading letters — every man can win
Some woman's love completely, had she won
My love as well! O what a monstrous world
Where such envenomed fire is, held by Chance
And shot in blindness. So she felt the flame
And looked on me, I felt the flame and looked
Upon this cockatrice.

        So as I said
I had been teacher, actor, writer, poet,
Had seen my face on lithographs, felt warm
In every capillary for that face
Which seemed star-guided, noble, to be loved,
Revered, and thus through self-esteem I bore
My failures hoping, buoyed by some success
As the swift years went by.

        But on a day
When I was forty-five, looked thirty-five,

MONSIEUR D—— TO THE PSYCHOANALYST

No gray hairs then, they called me thirty-five,
My name went round the city, in the press
They hailed me as a genius, I had played
Othello to their liking, was yet young
And promised much, they said.   That afternoon
A woman came to see me in my suite,
Wonder and admiration in her eyes.
Her manner halted, as she thumbed a book
Upon the table, while she told her tale:
She had won favor as an amateur,
Could I, the greatest talked of man to-day,
Show her the way to greatness, might it be
A modest part could be assigned to her
When I played mad Othello?

                    I have found
That when a woman has no business with you
Her calling speaks the oldest one of all.
So true to this I acted.   We commenced
And for three months I struggled for the prize.
Her first play was to make me pity her.
She told me of her suffering, her youth,
(She was then thirty-five), her poverty,
Her labor to learn French.   And like a man
I pitied her and opened up my purse.
She said, "No! No! this hat and dress will do,
It brushes well."   She would not take a cent.
I saw her daily for a month before

I won her.   Though she gave me hands and lips —
There was a fury in her lips, my heart
Seemed like to stop — I could not win the prize.
One day she broke in tears: "You seemed so noble,
So great of mind, are you then like the rest
Who want a woman's body, nothing else?"
"I want your love," I said, "your love for mine,
I love you, dearest!" faugh, must I repeat
The gagging words?   So I declared the love
I felt too deeply, and to prove my love
I added: "I'll renounce the gift of love,
My Lady Wonderful, worship you afar.
You would not have me tortured by your eyes,
Nor have me see you often, in this case!"
So I had given love as I had given
All wealth that I could pour of soul, achievement,
Name in the world, all pride, all thought of self
Present or future to this woman, now
For love's sake I renounced the gift of love.
And so I left her.   Well, she called me back.
And though I was a fool, and blinded too,
I saw her thought and won her in an hour.
So then commenced my madness, for she said
It could not be again.   The blood I tasted
Could not be drunk.   "You love me," she would say,
"Then bring me not to shame, it will be known
If we go on.   I cannot lose my bread.
Librarians cannot have their names in doubt

Who serve the public, as I do."   So it was
The madness braced my will, and unrelenting
I sought her, won her.   In a little while
We were adjusted to habitual love.
And I was happy save when I was mad.
For she knew younger men who came to call,
Or take her to the theatre, with one
She corresponded.   "Let it be," she said,
"I must not be in public with you, dear,
Whose name and greatness in the world would point
To our relationship, how could it be
You would be with a woman without station,
Celebrity or wealth, except for this?
These others are a blind."

                  I could not solve
Out of the whirling clouds of passion truth —
My days were tortured, in the dreams of sleep
I saw this dragon head I told you of.
And so through heavy venery, and dread,
And anger, doubt, faith, love and much of hate,
I took to drink.

              So drinking with her once,
For she could drink me blind, I turned and said:
"You say I am the first, I think you lie."
She wailed a flood of tears.   A hundred eyes
Turned on us in the café where we sat.

We left and walked the park.   I goaded her,
Pried out the secret.   Why, at twenty-three
She had become the mistress of a man.
It ended just six months before she came
To see me in my suite.

                Now here I was:
To hold on to myself I had to hold
This woman, win her wholly, crush her soul,
Destroy her so she would no longer be
My heart's desire.   For I had given all.
And I could see she valued it the less
As time went on.   My name, what was it now?
My art, what was it now?   She even hinted
I could not act Othello.   There was nothing
I could do more to keep her, hold her love,
Her admiration.   O how good esteem
Seems to a man who forfeits it to her
Whose body he can have, who cannot have
That sympathy whereby a man is nerved
To daily work and living.   What is Art?
No picture would be painted, poem sung
Save for the thought that woman close at hand,
Or somewhere in the world yet to be found
By reason of the picture or the poem,
Will see and love you for it.

                   Let me say
In passing, and dismiss it, I began

[254]

MONSIEUR D—— TO THE PSYCHOANALYST

With little sums until I gave her much.
There's matter of more moment.

                        I confess,
In spite of my licentious life, the creed
One sees among the artists, where I've lived,
To strong belief in woman's virtue, yes,
In spite of lip avowal of the faith
Of love called free, I have not quite believed it.
But it was in her soul.   She sucked that milk,
A child upon her mother's breast, she said —
It all came out at last from many talks,
And then, just then, I thought I saw foreshadowed
A social change upon the things of sex:
We read together Ann Veronica,
And Bernard Shaw, and laughed and said, at last
We see each other clearly.   We have found
A footing for our life.   I slept at last.
The dragon vanished from my dreams.   I waked
A song upon my lips, left drink alone,
Could face my image in the looking-glass,
And find restored a noble quality,
A strength and genius.

                    But if love be free
And if you love though only for an hour
Why not the cup of love?   Her former friend
Piqued to an interest by my love for her

Came back to see if he had overlooked
A beauty he would have.   Well, she confessed
Their night together.   It was at the time
My poor canzones which sang our stormy love
Had just been finished.   Every artist fool
Writes sonnets or canzones once in his life.
And so I had to add a verse to tell
Her faithlessness — or was it faithlessness ?
Since she declared she loved me, did not love
This older friend.   But if she did not love him
What was this act ?   She called it just a trial
Of our love which had stood the test, O God
Such mazes for my soul !

                              Flushed then with wrath
And drink I beat her cruelly.   She stood
With scarce a cry of pain and let me strike,
And said if I considered it was just
To beat her so, she wished to bear the pain.
Then with a cry I ceased.   We fell asleep
Stretched on the bed together.   When we woke
She kissed me her forgiveness.   I returned
The kiss, ah me !

                          So now the story turns.
There was a woman critic who pursued
My work with hateful words.   Before I knew
The cockatrice I found it best to fold

MONSIEUR D—— TO THE PSYCHOANALYST

This critic's column under, never read.
And in a day or two from that on which
I beat my mistress, what should I behold? —
A letter from her — she had left the town
Without my knowing, she was visiting
This critic enemy at her summer home.
And in this mail I found my poor canzones
Returned to me, and in the letter this:
"My friend says for some reason you would try
To compromise me by this wretched verse,
So I return it to you, go and burn.
I shall not see you more — so she advises,
And so I think.   I wish you well no less.
You are a little old to rise to fame,
Or excellence in acting, yet go on.
Perhaps there is not aught beside to do,
And it will occupy your mind, good-bye."

So shortly everywhere I seemed to sense
The feeling that they deemed me foul and base.
While we were friends I made her known to artists,
And writers in the city.   With this start
She had gone on and multiplied her friends
Among this folk.   I saw it all at once
As one sees dawn from darkness.   Then
The social standard melted, gave away
To all that had been written for some years.
Free love had won at last.   And we who kept

Our love in hiding, she who lied to keep
Her name as one who lived a maiden's life,
And I who doubted, hated her because
She was not freshly mine, we, she and I,
Stepped to a world all new, she to enjoy
And I to perish.   I was weak from loss
Of blood from wounds she gave me, spent for love
Poured for her sorrow, for she grieved and wept
That I was not her early love, her love
At love's beginning.   I went here and there
To build her life up, make it rich, repair
The injuries of her youth, retrieve the days
Which had brought loneliness.   Forbear with me —
I thought I could tell all in just a word —
Yes, this is it — She learned what was my strength
And took it for her own, found out my faults
And struck me there.   She gave me confidence
And trust, I fancied.   On analysis
She had concealed herself, there had not been
Clear understanding with us.   So she took
My friends, and friends are never wholly friends,
And made them hers, through these made other friends,
Explored my havens, my alliances,
My secret powers of prestige in the world.
And I awoke to find the world my foe!
And every desk of every editor
Silent for knowledge of me, breaking silence
In just a word of hate.   You see she loosed

MONSIEUR D—— TO THE PSYCHOANALYST

This story like a mist which creeps through cracks
That I had compromised her.   Then behold
I who had helped to bring this era in
Of sex equality, yes, in spite of all,
My ingrained feelings I have spoken of,
Found myself robbed of her by just the creed
I had upheld, and saw her live with him
Who was her friend, before I knew her, yes,
And justified by those whom she had feared,
Because they hated me, and pitied him
Bound to a woman in a loveless life
Who would not free him, let him marry her.

Then the last atom of my strength I summoned
To play Othello.   It was death or life!
Soul triumph or soul ruin.   But you see
The cockatrice had sent the word around
And sharpened every critic eye.   I faced
An audience of one mind, could sense it all
Where hatred, mild amusement were well mixed
To poison, paralyze creative power,
And even break my memory.   But I said
Show now your genius, drink the hatred in
Till all your spirit sparkles as a star
When the north wind of winter blows at night.
Nothing opposes but a woman's hate.
Rise on its wreckage.   So I spurred myself.
And even when I saw her critic friend

THE GREAT VALLEY

Limned from the mass of faces, lost my clue
And waited for the prompter, then my rage
Upheld me — yes, but wait — the rest is brief.

I had not acted through the strangle scene
When I heard calls and bells, the curtain fell,
My understudy led me from the stage.
Out in the night we went — I knew not where —
It was a night of drink, and I awoke
To strange surroundings in a scented room,
A woman with light hair lay by my side
"How did I get here" — then the woman laughed —
She was a Fury, for the Furies had me.
Out of the house I ran, from place to place,
All day went wandering in the city, thus
My wanderings of ten years began, they seem
Ten centuries.   What do you think of this?
I'm fifty-seven, with a bad complex,
Can you unravel it and make me well?

THE LAST CONFESSION

Dear, if you knew how my poor heart
Aches for your heart by day and night —
Forever lost to life's delight,
As seasons pass and years depart,
You would not let the invisible flame
Of hatred sear and scar your soul,
Where once in living light my name
Was lettered like an aureole!

You, who lost faith in me, will not
Believe this last confession, made
To lift your spirit from the shade
Wherein it walks and views the spot
Of my offense.   But when I saw
That our love's life must have an end,
I looked back o'er our path with awe
And traced it toward us to the sign
Where our ways severed, yours and mine.
There stood Remorse's dreaded shape!
Your Disbelief!   Your Self-Contempt!
I saw our love was not exempt
From ruin and could not escape.

THE GREAT VALLEY

We could not separate and smile,
And keep a faithful thought the while
Of understanding (like a spring
Hidden, refreshing, murmuring)
As friend sometimes takes leave of friend.
Then what was left? It was this thought
That at the last came forth to slay
Your love, without a warning brought
Ere my lips tightened to betray!

For as our love found depths too deep;
As absence almost deadened sense;
As often I awoke from sleep
And looked for hours at you, all tense,
Lest you awake and see my eyes,
Where the one thought of purest love
Shone like a fixed star's paradise,
I learned to know that Self above —
Making the heart's hierarchy pure —
Stands the archangel Truth, preferred —
Throned over Love which can endure
Only where Truth has stood, unstirred.
Watchful and with his torch of stars
Held o'er Love's face, although it shows
The forehead's pain, the bosom's scars,
The cheeks bleached out from secret tears
In memory of impalpable blows,
Shed in the night's long solitude.

THE LAST CONFESSION

You see I could not give you truth!
There was the Shadow in my life
Cast by the fierce Sun of my youth.
And as our day fell to the west
The Shadow lengthened and the strife
'Twixt Love and Truth within my breast
Waxed fiercer.   Heaven's deathless blue
Leaned on my hungering soul and pained
Its wings, as if a joy were lost,
Or never had been quite attained,
Or captured at too great a cost.
I could not give you truth all true.
My love for you and then the thirst
For all your love, made me accursed
Of fear that if you knew me first,
Just as I am, your heart would cease
To cherish mine.   And then much more
Was this fear venom to my peace
When all the world spread out before
Our astonished eyes, as our own world,
And we its children, each for each.

This was the sleepless worm which curled
In my heart's petals, at the root
Where my heart's sweetness had its source.
You never saw the worm!   My speech
Poised like a bee who knows the loot
Of honey's gone, and turns his course.

THE GREAT VALLEY

I kept the petals closed, and you
Breathed at their tips, but would have known
All of their fragrance, or of blight.
That's love — to have no place where light
And understanding have not shone.
Your face reproached me — I who knew
No sweet or bitter essences
Can be withheld from Love that keeps
An onward flight, which ever sees,
Or would see, all in the heart's deeps.

Then Life came, and with lifted sword
Laid on our souls his dread command;
"Say your farewells, part hand from hand,
You the adorer, and adored.
Duty is seeking you!   And Grief
Would have her child return and see
The changeless halls of Misery,
And the bare board and darkened hearth."
I reeled with anguish as the earth
Sank from my feet.   For oh the end
Seemed far as death!   And when it came
It was my hope, my soul's desire
To part as friend may part from friend,
And that you'd keep alive my name
Bright as an altar's quenchless fire.
It could not be!   How could it be?
I was not truth!   I was not true —

THE LAST CONFESSION

I kept my soul's real self from you.
Then I bethought me: "Since his earth
Is Autumn-stricken with a doubt
That I am worth not his love's worth,
Were it no better he should know
Disloyalty made definite
By a suspected past re-knit,
And see our love a play played out,
Than to live through the soft decline
Of our bright day to solemn eve —
A sunset of remembrance — where
He walks devoured by love and hate —
Love for the love I strove to give,
Hate for a thought intuitive:
Some newer love her heart hath won
Or some first love hath won her back.
No, to my faith, he says, "I'll cleave,
Believing that I can't believe."
"Slow death to love!   Exquisite rack!"
Ah me! I had not made this fate —
The warp was stretched, the woof was spun,
The roof-tree laid long years before
You entered at the unbolted door.
"Then what is best?   What can be done?
To give him back his pride and strength,
And even his peace of mind at length?
Better a quick blow!   Better blood!
To brace the soul and poise the brain

And make him what he was again."
Just then the Shadow near me stood
Who stepped aside for you.   He took
With unabated comradeship
My hand in his.   That closed our book.
I woke to hear the water drip
Blown out of heavens low and dim.
He brushed my tears off with his hand —
Nor clouds nor memory trouble him.
And my one thought of you was this:
I've cured you with this sacrifice —
The hate has come to you I planned.
The hate that may take form in words,
For scorn like this: "I found a seam
"Right at the contact of our love.
"No recreative fire can warm
"And fuse fine gold with lifeless dross,
"Or worthy metal make thereof."
This killed your love and wrecked your dream!
This is my soul's confession.   Wait,
A trickster in a hooded form
Stands by as we begin to pull
The weaving beam, and throws between
The warp and woof a ball of wool.
It catches and is woven in
The colors, spoils the conscious blend,
Changes the pattern to the end.
Whatever it be I call it fate.

THE LAST CONFESSION

In misery or in happiness
We must live on awhile no less.
Shall we be master weavers, climb,
Or leave the loom, or waste the time?
Or guide the shuttle till the threads
Weave clear or turn to worthless shreds?

IN THE LOGGIA

There were seven nights of the moon
This August, beloved.
There were nights before the seven
When we scarcely saw the moon,
Or perhaps as we canoed, ere the sun sank,
We saw her as a transparent tissue of white
Against a sky as white.
But when we first saw the moon
She had risen before the sun had sunk.
Then the next night she was brighter
With the evening planet above her,
Despite the tongues of fire in the west
Where the sun had set on fire
Great coils of cloud!
And then there were those nights between
Her growth and her o'erflowing fullness
When hand in hand we walked in your garden
Amid the Chinese balloons and coreopsis,
Hibiscus, marigold, hydrangeas,
Under the rose arches,
And by the hedge of California privet,
And looked at the lake,

IN THE LOGGIA

And the moon in the sky
And the moon on the lake.

And do you remember what we saw
As we stared at the wake of the moon
On the lake?
The ripples made blacknesses,
And the moon made silver splendors,
And as we stared we saw
In the shadows of waves
Running into the light of the moon on the water
Youths and maids and children
Coming from darkness into the light in a dance,
Joining hands, falling into embraces,
Hurrying to evanishment at the path of light
Where the moon had paved the water.
I shall never see the moon on the water
Without seeing these youths and maids and children,
And without thinking of that night
Of the full moon!

This was the night
We saw the moon rise, from the very first,
Across the lake o'ertopping the forest.
A spire of pine stood up
Against a sky made pale as of the northern lights.
But in a moment a bit of fire lit the spire of the pine
As it were a candle lighted.

THE GREAT VALLEY

And she rose so fast that I took my watch
To time the rising of the moon
Free and clear of the spire.
And she rose so fast that as we gazed
She cleared the spire,
And soared with such silent glory above the forest,
And sailed to the southwest of the spire.
And at that moment the whippoorwills
Began to sing in the woodlands near —
We had not heard them before in all this summer.
And we stood in the loggia
In the silence of our own thoughts,
In the silence of the full moon!

And it was then that the pressure of your hand
Gave me a meaning of sorrow.
It was then that the pressure of your hand
Spoke, as flame which turns in the wind,
Of a change in your heart.
But if not a change, of another's heart
Toward whom you turned.

And I sit in the loggia to-night
Waiting for the moon to rise,
She will not rise till midnight,
And then she will rise, a poor half wreck of herself.
No whippoorwill has sung to-night,
And none will sing.

IN THE LOGGIA

And if there are youths and maids and children
Hurrying into the dance on the water,
Embracing and fading in light,
I shall not see.
No, in this darkness where I breathe
The scent of the sweet alyssum
Which you planted and tended
I shall wait for midnight,
And the rise of our ruined moon.

In the darkness of the loggia
Under a sky that hopes for no moon to-night,
Save the wasted moon of midnight,
I am filled with a deep happiness
And a thankfulness to the Power
Behind the sky:
I am filled with a joy as wide and deep as nature
That my love for you
Can live without your love for me,
And asks nothing of you,
And nothing for you
Save that you find what you seek!

BE WITH ME THROUGH THE SPRING

The snow has passed, the crocus blooms,
A swelling tide of life returns;
Green lights invade the forest glooms,
All nature wakes and yearns.
The breeze lifts and the ships take wing
To havens which we long have known;
And yet — and yet I dread the spring,
For fear you may be gone.

Life gives us sweet delights and then
Gathers them back and buries them deep.
Oh, wanton hearts, that kill them when
They do not tire or sleep.
The breeze lifts and the ships take wing —
Be with me through the spring.

DESOLATE SCYTHIA

Χθονὸς μεν ἐς τηλουρὸν ἤκομεν πεδον. — AES.

When there are no distances in music,
No far off things suggested of faery forests or celestial
    heights ;
When nothing undiscovered stands back of the written
    page,
And the landscape contains nothing hidden,
And no alluring spirits of further places ;
When no more in eyes shines the light of mystery,
And the thrill of discovered kinships
Has fallen into the familiar recognition
That takes all men and women
As daily associates of an accustomed world,
Then you have come to the uttermost plain of earth
Where lie the rocks of desolate Scythia.

THE SEARCH

When the hill grows green at midway time,
And bronze buds toss in the lane
It is sweet to follow the river swallow
Where the tiles are red from rain.

When the slanting wind shakes apple blossoms,
And the willow trees are bowed
The balcony banners flutter up
Where sails the hilltop cloud.

The balcony banners are ever the same
Wherever the heart may stray;
One sports the tiger and one the dragon
Whether you weep or play.

Where Little Boy Blue and the Knave of Hearts
And the Goose Girl dance on the green;
Where Knights in red and gold ride forth
Guarding the King and Queen;

Where the glint of swords is the only light
On a passing storm of men;
Or where the Furies rocking wait
For the world to die again;

THE SEARCH

Where horsemen ride by the winding river
Galloping in the quest:
One wears black and one wears yellow,
And one in red is dressed.

One fares in the flaunt of a scholar's cloak,
And a velvet hat and plume;
Two ride with eyes fixed on the ground,
And one with a face of gloom.

One laughs at the others and laughs at himself,
Two think of themselves alone;
One sees a goal for his thirsting soul,
And life as a stepping stone.

They pass through a village where
Some boys are flying kites.
The people come with food and wine
To entertain the Knights.

And one takes bread and one takes cake,
Three drink a little wine.
And two drink for their heart's delight,
And one for an anodyne.

And the Knight in red slips off to a tavern
And drinks him deep and strong,
And then he hurries to catch his fellows
And hails them with a song.

THE GREAT VALLEY

They come to a village that lay
Within a King's domains:
The Knight in yellow takes his sword
And strikes away the chains.

They come to a place of festival
Through which there passed a hearse:
The Knight in black reins in his steed
To look thereon and curse.

They come to a hall of curious books
Under a mountain peak:
The Knight in the scholar's cloak goes in
And talks with them in Greek.

And all the way by the winding river
By heaven's breeze unfurled
The tiger banner and dragon banner
Flutter around the world.

As night drew down they come to a palace
Of laughter, lights and din.
Says the Knight in red, "I tarry here,
For I hear the violin."

"Nay," says the Knight in yellow dressed;
"Nay," says the Knight in black;
"Nay," says the scholar, "I sleep in the open
To study the Zodiac."

THE SEARCH

Out comes to them an equerry
And sees their piteous dole:
"Come in," says the ruddy equerry,
"And dine with Old King Cole."

He seized their horses ere they could turn
And led them where candles shone,
And there with a crown tipped on his head
Sat the monarch on his throne.

"What is your name, all yellow dight,
And where does your sovereign reign?"
The sorrowful Knight then answered the King:
"I'm traveling back to Spain."

"What is your name, all dressed in black,
And whither do you roam?"
"I was a mad prince they sent to England
And now I'm going home."

"What is your name, in a scholar's cloak,
And what is your heart's joy?"
"I search through Europe night and day
For a spouse for Helen of Troy."

"They're as mad as hatters," said King Cole
As he straightened his crown on his head.
"Go call in the fiddlers, bring my bowl,
Fetch me my pipe," he said.

"But hold," said Cole, "who are you, fellow,
"Now answer me fair and well?"
"I was born in France," said the Knight in red,
"And my name's Pantagruel."

"That's a good name," laughed old King Cole.
"But whither are you bound?"
"I search for the Holy Bottle, King,
"And I pray it may be found."

"That's a true answer," said Old King Cole,
"And here you shall abide;
"Come up to my throne and reign forever,
"And sit you by my side."

"Away with the rest," said Old King Cole,
"And fetch my bowl," said he.
"Here is Pantagruel found at last,
"To keep me company."

From under the throne he drew the bottle
And poured wine into the bowl;
Pantagruel stepped to the dais
And drank with Old King Cole.

"Give yellow and black and scholar's cloak
A bed in the royal room."
But Old King Cole and Pantagruel
Drank till the morning's bloom.

THE SEARCH

They laughed and drank till the dawn was red,
While the sleepers prayed and wept.
They sang to the violins till day,
While black and yellow slept.

But Old King Cole, the merry old soul,
Was a curious soul as well:
"Who are these fellows," queried he
Of his friend Pantagruel.

"Well, never ask me," said Pantagruel,
"I met them down by the river;
"But whether they came from the Land of Lanterns
"They're traveling on forever."

They went to the room with a candle light
And looked in the face of the three —
"They're a sorry lot," said Old King Cole;
"They're a sorry lot," said he.

They held the candle to gray beard's face,
And gray beard moaned in his rest.
And pricked in color of India ink
Was a windmill on his breast.

The other muttered "Life is a shadow,"
And his face was young and pale:
And pricked on his arm was a green serpent
Devouring its own tail.

The other sighed: "I still must struggle
And strive until I die."
And over his heart was pricked the shape
Of a wingéd butterfly.

"What do I see," said Old King Cole,
"Has the wine gone into my brain?
"Who's Helen of Troy? Who'd leave England?
"And who'd return to Spain?"

Pantagruel and Old King Cole
Slip down the stairs in stealth,
They fill the bowl from the Holy Bottle
And drink each other's health.

They stand at the window to watch the sun
And the mists of morning clear:
Three knights on horses climb the hill,
And silently disappear.

And yellow and black and scholar's cloak
Into the light have gone;
And the tiger banner and dragon banner
Flutter against the dawn.

There's the dragon banner," says Old King Cole,
"And the tiger banner," he sighs.
Pantagruel breaks into a laugh,
As the monarch dries his eyes.

[280]

Printed in the United States of America.

THE following pages contain advertisements of books by the same author or on kindred subjects.

By RABINDRANATH TAGORE

Author of " Sadhana," " The King of the Dark Chamber," etc.

Fruit Gathering

Perhaps of all Tagore's poetry the most popular volume is " Gitanjali." It was on this work that he was awarded the Nobel Prize in Literature. These facts lend special interest to the announcement of this book, which is a sequel to that collection of religious " Song Offerings." Since the issue of his first book, some four years ago, Tagore has rapidly grown in popularity in this country, until now he must be counted among the most widely read of modern poets. Another volume of the merit, the originality, the fine spiritual feeling of " Gitanjali " would even further endear him to his thousands of American admirers.

The Hungry Stones and Other Stories

Some of the more notable of Mr. Tagore's short stories are here presented in translations by the author and with illustrations by native Indian artists. Ernest Rhys, in his biography of Tagore, devotes much space to a consideration of him as a short story writer, advancing the opinion that this particular form of literature is one of the most important expressions of Tagore's genius. Now for the first time English readers are given the opportunity of acquainting themselves with the new Tagore and of forming their own estimate of him. None of the material in this volume has ever appeared before in English.

THE MACMILLAN COMPANY

Publishers   **64–66 Fifth Avenue**   **New York**

NEW MACMILLAN POETRY

The New Poetry. An Anthology

EDITED BY HARRIET MONROE AND ALICE CORBIN HENDERSON, Editors of Poetry

Probably few people are following as closely the poetry of to-day as are the editors of the *Poetry Magazine* of Chicago. They are eminently fitted, therefore, to prepare such a volume as this, which is intended to represent the work that is being done by the leading poets of the land. Here, between the covers of one book, are brought together poems by a great many different writers, all of whom may be said to be responsible in a measure for the revival of interest in poetry in this country. The volume is unusual, not only in the number of names which it contains, but in the splendid insight which it gives into a literature which seems to be coming once more into its own.

Poems of the Great War

BY J. W. CUNLIFFE

Here are brought together under the editorship of Dr. Cunliffe some of the more notable poems which have dealt with the great war. Among the writers represented are Rupert Brooke, John Masefield, Lincoln Colcord, William Benet, Wilfrid Wilson Gibson, Hermann Hagedorn, Alfred Noyes, Rabindranath Tagore, Walter De La Mare, Vachel Lindsay and Owen Seaman.

THE MACMILLAN COMPANY

Publishers   64–66 Fifth Avenue   New York